Why Discrimination?

The agony of an immigrant, who just wanted to be kind and do his job

William Anthony

Why Discrimination?

ISBN-13: 978-1518871641
ISBN-10: 151887164X

DEDICATION:

To my endowment with such qualities of character, spirit and mind.

INDEX

ACKNOWLEDGMENTS

I would like to express my gratitude to those who have been of help, to those who have adviced me and to those who have commented on the manuscript. I also want to thank Franklin Dominico (Boi) Antoin for the cover image, Gert Oostindie for bringing me in contact with a group wonderful people, Debra Forthman, Ph.D. for the applause and James Dryden for showing a bit of his editing. I am very grateful to Daan Nijssen who corrected the English with dedication.

And also thanks for the lovely compliments:

"This looks like an interesting story ... I was drawn in by your tone and honesty and wanted to find out more about what happened." – Jane Edwards;

"You have an important story to tell, and I would be honored to help you ..." – Laura Kenney;

"... you have a lot of strength, determination, and heart." – Andrew;

"Your work seems very interesting and is written in a very lively fashion. Best wishes." – Rosemary Robson.

Many thanks to all of you.

INTRODUCTION

This story is written from my artistic and creative qualities. The judge named them qualities of character, spirit and mind. I consider the statement of the Tribunal as praise to my personal characteristics, although by definition this is not what you call a "nice story." It's about discrimination, a form of discrimination which we wish no longer existed in the Netherlands, but in our hearts, we know better. I have personally experienced how it is still very much alive, and I wrote this book.

In the period 1988—1993 I was employed at the municipal public transport service in Amsterdam, the GVB. That's where it all happened. The content of this book is based on reports, letters, decisions of the judicial authorities, and other documents.

As carefully as possible, I give the facts of the complaint, how the GVB dealt with the decision of the commission, how it thought to resolve the discriminatory treatment after the first notice of dismissal and what the judge has said of the second dismissal notice. The GVB interpreted that legal decision incorrectly, as the judge said that they should have done it in a different way. And the third dismissal decision was a hit. According to the court, it was up to the unfavorable circumstances in which I found myself.

The civil employment agreement also comes up at the end. This was next to the permanent appointment as public servant. In 2010, I brought it to the courts, again showing the quality of character, spirit and mind that I possess.

Discrimination and racism in the Netherlands are difficult to investigate and understood through numbers. However, in different ways, anti-discrimination agencies try to collect data on discrimination and racism.
It is hidden. And in my opinion, a kind of weakness.

1. WILL YOU BE ONE OF US?

There was an ambitious recruitment campaign going on for subway inspectors: "Will you be one of our 100 new cabin stewards?" I often traveled by subway and watched the inspectors doing their job. These were not always the most pleasant moments, but still … The inspectors would stop and chat with the passengers – a talk here and there – and where necessary fine a fare dodger. It seemed to me a nice job so I responded to the ad.

I was cordially invited to attend an information meeting on Monday, January 11, 1988. The meeting focused on a number of topics: the public transport company as an employer, the contents of the job and the training. There was a slide show. I listened intently and looked around the room. I had already noticed a light-skinned woman who was now standing nearby. She was the one to whom I had to report earlier, when I had first arrived. I'd met her once before at one of the seminars at the Open University and now I discovered that she was working for the subway on the Human Resources Department. Her name was Tanya. An appointment was made for an interview on January 14, 1988, with the head staff. I was asked to take along a number of documents, including diplomas, certificates etc. Perhaps it would have been better not to have mentioned that I was doing a basic course in Dutch law. The person in charge of the selection seemed unimpressed.

"Somewhere we have to delineate," he said and suggested that it might be better if I continued with my studies.

"I study employment law," he added.

I guess what he meant was that they probably had to set a limitation to the qualification—or something else—of the candidates. Another man dressed in a blue uniform was sitting at the table but said nothing. The interview lasted about 45 minutes and ended with the usual comment: "You will hear from us." I left the hall. The man in charge of the selection process came hurrying after me. He said something like: "You shouldn't do it. These people are ..." He left the sentence hanging in the air. It seemed like they didn't want me to go any further and to withdraw the application procedure. But why? All that was required was an education level set at MAVO / LTS-C. I had more than that. So what was the problem?

A few days later I received a call for a medical examination on Monday, April 18, 1988, at the Company Health Service in the monumental Scheepvaarthuis (Shipping House) in Amsterdam, the headquarters of the Municipal Transport Company of Amsterdam (GVB). I was present in good time and went to the Human Resources department, where I received a form on which I had to fill in some information needed for the medical examination. So far, so good. I did not suspect there was a surprise waiting for me.

My hearing and eyesight were checked. Everything was fine. Finally, I would be examined by the medical examiner. When I entered his room, I didn't see who he was right away. I took off my clothes—except for the underwear—and sat down on a bed. The doctor gave a few taps on my knees and asked: "How is Onno?" I sat up straight and thought: "Who is this again?" Right then I remembered him. For me it was a pleasant surprise, but apparently not for him. His body language spoke volumes.

It was Peter. A couple of weeks prior to the examination Onno and I had visited him at his house. That visit didn't last long, however. We hadn't yet properly entered the house, when we were directed out again. Onno and Peter knew each other. Peter had a drag act in Onno's 'Antonie Theater'. Anyway, we had a common friend, so the medical exam will be fine, or so I thought.

"Do you practice any sports?" he asked.

"No." I replied.

"Unhealthy," he said.

It felt a bit like a cold shower, but still I didn't notice anything hostile in him against me. I would be confronted with that much later.

After the medical check-up, a psychological examination was planned. That was the next day, January 15. The selector—with whom I had the interview—was prominently present at the Public Health Service of Amsterdam (GGD) on that day. He spoke to me and this time he was clear. Just before the test began, he asked if I wanted to withdraw the application process. I had indicated quite clearly to him, that I had no reason to do so. Since I came from Curaçao, I had been living off of unemployment benefits. I still had my WW-payments, but I only had a few months to go until I would end up on welfare. That was what I wanted to avoid. Not so much because of the low income, but the idea itself was not pretty to me: living on social security at such an early stage of my life—as if I were incompetent.

So why would I let myself be discouraged by this man? I did the test. Afterwards I had a conversation in a separate room with one of the senior staff members in charge of the project. The selector was there again as well.

"You have done it anyway, huh?" he said.

And I said: "Yeah."

On January 19, 1988, the written report of the psychological examination was sent to the GVB. The result was not that bad at all for me. "His intellectual capacities are sufficient for the position" the psychologist wrote. However, he also wrote that I didn't fully meet the requirements for the job and that I had somewhat of a problem with handling tensions. Note the 'somewhat'. Anyway, I hadn't been connected to a cable or device to measure any tension.

The selector, his name was Ton, called me the same day with the announcement that the medical examiner, Peter, had rejected me from the application process because, according to him, there would be problems related to my health in the foreseeable future. I was surprised and I sure wanted to know what kind of problems the crystal ball of Peter was predicting, but I got no answer on the telephone. Still, I did not give up. The same day I sent an objection to the GVB, in which I protested against the rejection. Was this the beginning of a harassment campaign? Did the selector feel as if his toes had been stepped on? Possibly someone at the GVB was pretty pissed off.

ENTIE

Personeel van de Amsterdamse metro in vergadering bijeen. Er dreigden donderdag opnieuw acties, nadat er woensdagavond was ingebroken in twee ruimtes waar kaartjes voor de metro werden verkocht. Foto Bert Verhoeff

2. BLACKBITE

At last, I got the job: a fixed-term civil contract for one year. Nevertheless, I still had to do the necessary effort, such as writing an objection letter against this rejection without a valid reason. In the letter I wrote to the GVB that the rejection was in conflict with the general principles of good governance. My law degree study couldn't be expected to have such an impact on future colleagues that their functioning would be disturbed and the interest of the municipality would be harmed. I considered the underlying motivation for my rejection as an infringement on the obligation to state reasons (*motiveringsbeginsel*). The written and unwritten rules of public law also apply to private law actions of governing bodies - HR 27-03-1987, NJ 1987, 727 Amsterdam/Ikon [*Supreme Court*]. In the letter I didn't mention Peter's crystal ball. Ton could tell them more about that himself. Later on, I saw in my personnel file that the Cabin Stewards supervisor had conducted the research on my letter on January 19, 1988. There was indeed no valid reason to reject my application. This could be inferred from the letter stating that, starting from April 18, 1988, I could start working at the municipal transport company.

On that day I was present at 8:30 AM in the Scheepvaarthuis. The contract had already been signed on April 12 on behalf of the Mayor of Amsterdam. There were only a few formalities left to do, like a photo shoot and picking up the keys. After that, the training Special Investigation Officer Passenger Transport Act.—also known as

Revenue Control Inspector (Bijzonder Opsporingsambtenaar Wet personenvervoer)—began. I successfully completed the training, which took about seven weeks.

The recruitment of new cabin stewards was part of a project to maintain safety in trams, buses and metro, to provide information to passengers and to check for valid tickets. Security, Information, Control: the VIC-project. A government project of the Ministry of Transport, Ministry of Justice and the four public transport companies, the Amsterdam GVB, RET Rotterdam, HTM the Hague and West Netherlands. The goal was to achieve a reduction of black and gray traveling (fare dodging), a decrease in vandalism and an improvement of the safety and information to passengers. Besides that, the VIC project aimed to contribute to the fight against unemployment, especially among young people belonging to ethnic minorities. The VICs were recruited from unemployed people in the age group between 22 and 33 years with a low level of education. Some had not even completed earned a diploma. The project did make an important contribution in the fight against unemployment and the integration of women and ethnic minorities in employment. (Andel, H. G. Van, M. Hoekert - van Der Wind, and C. A. De Jongh. Veiligheid, Informatie, Controle in Het Openbaar Vervoer: Eindevaluatie Vic-project. [Security, Information, Control in Public Transport: Final evaluation Vic project.] 's-Gravenhage: Ministerie Van Verkeer En Waterstaat, 1987. Print.)

For variety, there was another task, which was to keep an eye on the stops, to make sure that all equipment is operating properly and to sell tickets. I also completed the training for station officer successfully. Despite the ups and downs surrounding the solicitation procedure, things started out all right. I received the 'Ordinance of Appointing an

Investigating Officer'. The appointment to office followed in July 1988, in the District Court at Parnassusweg in Amsterdam. After that I officially became an authorized VIC'er.

Shortly after finishing the VIC'er traject, there was a vacancy for the position of metro driver / station official. I applied for the position, but was rejected. The reason was that I didn't comply with the requirement of "a high degree of employability for a longer period." Excuse me, how so? It was again an argument of the same type as the one at my first application. I had hoped that this kind of nonsense was behind me now. I thought it would be better not pay attention to it anymore. With a crystal ball, I would still have nothing. I had only been employed recently, I did not know much about the company culture yet and my employment was for only one year. In other words, it was better to avoid further conflicts as much as possible.

Summer was coming on and it was vacation time. There was quite a cozy atmosphere: a whole group at work on the subway. We were brand new, so we were very eager to work. In our blue suits we left the station at the Weesperplein in a "bang it" mood. In July, I received a short performance evaluation. It was made by an authorized officer. It did not appear to be an official one, but everything turned out to be sufficient. For administration, I even got a sufficient-plus. I was extremely happy with the job and I thought I had finally found the rest that I needed in order to proceed with my law studies. Despite the bustle of the work, I managed to do an exam in April. During the quiet station duty I could find the time to study the other modules. However, the question was for how long. Some colleagues became very interested in my private life, but I felt no desire to share my private affairs with anybody and I certainly wasn't interested in their opinions about what I was doing.

I could understand them very well. Their problems, circumstances and background. They were people who had been unemployed for a long time and who had now received a job through the government's help. Still, this was a sensitive issue, especially when it came to the position of foreigners. A recurring topic was the political discussion about the introduction of a so-called Allochtone Consultation Board. This consultation board developed activities that were directed against racism, discrimination of ethnic minorities within the GVB. With special campaigns and selection procedures, allochtones were given preferential treatment when recruiting staff. This was also called 'affirmative action' and 'positive discrimination'. Selected immigrants (allochtones) often disappeared too quickly; the so-called revolving door effect. Some white colleagues had a problem with that positive discrimination policy. Others didn't want to be categorized as immigrant. Especially the mixed-race. A person from these ethnic minority groups is referred to as an allochthone in Dutch political rhetoric.

At first I didn't recognize a link between the establishment of the Immigrants (allochthone) Consultation Board and the accusation of a colleague at my address. It was not that clear to me. I wasn't even a part of the Consultation Board. Nevertheless, in a letter from the crew chief to the chief Cabin Supervisors it appears that the colleague Inge Van Daalen—in a sly report—accused me of dropping the charges of foreigners who were fare dodging. It looked like a targeted attack on me, because the next day she wrote another report. And so the nagging began...

These reports were kept in a 'secret' file. I was not allowed to read them. By hearsay I came to know about it. Barely a week later—after Van Daalen's second 'report'—at the request of some VIC'ers led by

Ger Verdam, a meeting was held about my behavior at work. Verdam was a close friend of Van Daalen. The core of the problem seemed to have been related to the giving of actual assistance if problems were to arise during the checks in the metro or at the stations. Verdam wanted to know if I was willing to fight if necessary. I indicated very clearly that I distanced myself from all forms of violence, especially if violence was apparently provoked. The team chief reported this to the chef Wagon Supervisors and added:

"Also there would be a matter of pardoning passengers of ethnic groups; report Van Daalen, September 11 and 12, 1988. Despite all the allegations Mr. Anthony continues to be serviceable, calm and restrained. He performs assigned tasks and responsibilities without contradiction and doubt."

3. IF YOU DON'T LIKE IT ...

Apparently Verdam and his friends were not satisfied with the outcome of the conversation. They continued making their allegations. It started to look like a reign of terror in the making. One of them said that if I did not like how things were going, I could better leave. I felt cornered.

In November my civil employment contract would be terminated prematurely. It would be changed into a temporary Civil Servants appointment in accordance with the ARA, Amsterdam Public Personnel Regulation, and I would become an official. Still, the continued nagging of these people put even this possibility of a permanent appointment at the Municipality Amsterdam at risk. Herman de Beer—shift leader Cabin Stewards—became desperate. He did not know what to do with the flow of complaints. I had no other choice than to consult the company's confidante, Maureen Vreede. She was of Surinamese descent and appointed by the Deputy Director, also of Surinamese descent, to bring racism and discrimination at the GVB in sight. When they heard that the confidante would come for a conversation, the bullying stopped suddenly. In October, the confidante spoke with the team chief and made a record of that conversation. "No, I don't think this is a matter of 'discrimination', only of a disturbed working relationship." the supervisor opined. "I will investigate the matter from my own expertise and give guidance", he promised. He continued: "Sir Anthony is a good employee, but he hardly allied himself to others. Whenever something happens to him, he thinks too much and too long about it. He will have to adapt. The fact that he had heard from a colleague that 'if he doesn't like it here, he can better go' will be rectified." The confidante: "Was the group satisfied with the conversation?" Chief: "It's true that the entire group wasn't satisfied. But I will come back to it." The confidante expressed her hope for a positive outcome. She would welcome any new ways of approach and possible solutions of the shift supervisor.

The action was like a bomb blast, as it turned out. It was impossible to fight alone against that established group without help from outside. There was another intense period coming up, which also needed urgent attention of the company. Often burglaries were committed at the metro stations where we sold the tickets for the subway. Since we were travelling with cash and tickets during the evenings—in the dark sometimes—there was a risk of being personally robbed. For that reason, the management of the GVB had decided to temporarily stop the sale of tickets at the metro stations. In addition, the public service union had announced actions if things weren't going to change. As the Volkskrant wrote on Friday, October 14, 1988: "Information meeting in the CVL (Central Traffic Control) building as result of burglaries in metro station areas." Guess who featured in front on the published photo? ME!

There also was the issue about my appointment as a cabin steward. What was it going to be? Temporary appointment, tenure or the end? A permanent appointment was not the talk of the day yet. In November, the supervisor wrote to the confidante that at that time, no negative signals about me had been detected, but shortly after the letter had been sent, Van Dam announced that he would request a new meeting with the leadership, in which he wanted to bring up my sex life. This could have a bad influence on the team, according to him.

Instead of his personal attacks on me, it would be much better if that guy could deal with more urgent problems at work, like burglaries at metro stations, vindictive passengers who did not hesitate to spit a controller in the face, and some pugnacious colleagues who liked to "bang it out". These kinds of things were more important, in my opinion, than rooting in someone's private life; about whether I shared the bed with a man or a woman or about 'how we did it in bed.' I refused to talk about my private life. I had no desire to talk about my personal life with anyone, especially when I was forced to do it.

It looked like Verdam had an urge to prove something to one or more people. But what? And to whom? His new request for an interview about me was honored by the team chief. It was held in a local station at Bullewijk. That it would be about me was obvious and that Verdam did not feel at ease was also noticeable. He didn't dare to say what exactly was going on according to him. After some twisting and growling he said: "I want to be transferred to squad 7." This was the team that his friends were in; among others Van Daalen and her boyfriend. "I feel that I'm fitting in much better there." he argued. The team chief rejected that request: "You are not going to group 7 and this group 3 will not be a mirror of it. No one here will be the scapegoat." Verdam also said that he did not feel safe and wanted to be equipped with a baton and a gun to get the job done properly. He wanted to know what I thought of the idea, and once again I told him what I thought of the use of force in public transport. Little by little, the conversation progressed, although it was still mostly about my private affairs. A colleague of Indo-Surinamese origin; Laura Ferrier—who was new in the team—took over. She wanted to imitate how I moved and made exaggerated feminine gestures. "I don't want to be seen 'like that' by the public." she said. "I must also walk in that monkey suit."

The team chef chopped her down immediately and said: "I have to wear the monkey suit too."

Verdam maintained his objections. "I firmly have a problem with it." he said. He suggested a round of voting.

The team chief sat straight up stiffly.

4. REPORTS, REPORTS

There was more going on. I had received a message from squad 7 that my teammates had trouble with me always being absorbed in the books. "The opportunity to develop yourself is one of the Human Rights." I uttered. "What Human Rights?" Ger Verdam asked. "We also have rights." He meant that he and some of his friends were lacking legal protection. In other words, the investigating officer also had to be wary with his bashing.

That Yvonne Waal thought of me as a hoity-toity with my nose in the air because of my law study, was not new to me. Earlier, she had come to the station with her Surinamese friend and both had attempted to tear pages out of my laws bundle. I could avoid this only by standing on the books and putting them in a bag. It was said that some of the team chiefs wanted to have the Criminal Code in their office. When I heard of that I made a cynical remark: "As far as I'm concerned, they can set up an entire legal filing in the office." Another example of this was that of a guy who always played his keyboard in the office. It was really a hilariously unpretty situation. Such posturing and pettiness—which began to get management support—were a revelation to me. I would not call them narrow minded, but rather people who just begrudge others; the wannabes, wannahaves and me-too freeloaders. There is a Japanese saying: "The nail that sticks out gets hammered down."

After his laudatory letter two months before, the team leader wrote in a new letter to the chief Cabin Supervisors, Jan Green: "Understanding for and acceptance of the view of colleagues, insight and adaptability are not sufficient. As Mr. Anthony persists in his conduct, the problems appear to be largely due to himself." It was a 180 degree turn on behalf of the chief. The bursting bubble became visible to me, but it weren't their own bubbles they were bursting. I couldn't understand why I had to live up to the group's standards. Was it just to meet their perception? To fulfill their illusion? Why should I accept them pigeonholing me?

What Ton, the selector, probably meant with his sentence was becoming clear to me. It involved a certain mentality: a mentality of interfering with other people's private lives, of thinking that others should have a way of life that is acceptable to them, and of imposing it by force, if needed, of spending hours gossiping about me based on their preconceived opinion. In my mailbox an erotic picture of a few men with erections had been left. Someone wrote on it: "Which one do you want?" I handed the photo to the chief of service. There would be an investigation. As far as I know, it was never carried out.

I couldn't quite figure out De Beer; the shift supervisor. He was playing both the good and the bad guy. A few days after the conversation at Bullewijk I again received a perception note. Motivation, handling tickets, attitude towards passengers, attitude towards colleagues, appearance and clothing; everything was rated perfect. It seemed that peace had returned. Occasionally some inappropriate comments were made, but I could live with it. After the busy and heavy month of December, the beginning of the new year was a relief to me. Almost everyone was very kind. Or were they simply pretending to be friendly?

In any case, I had to get the drive again. I called the Central Participation Committee (CMC) to organize the election for a representative of the team. The election was held on January 9, 1989. Verdam was elected as a team representative and a secretary of staff meetings, and I was appointed as a reserve representative. That was the revival of the official team 3 work meetings.

The entire month of January went well; even between Verdam and me. He became quiet. We prepared the team meetings together, we discussed some issues and we understood each other. That was until Waalders was assigned to the group; only for one whole shift. She made it clear to everyone who was the boss. Of course, she still had problems with my presence and my study. At certain moments the work was once again interrupted. We had to go to the office for a talk, because Waalders wanted to. The reason? I went to the bathroom and missed a metro. Even when I was talking to someone by phone my voice was annoying Waalders. She felt as if I ignored her. I tried to explain to her that whenever she was talking to others about their children and dogs, I didn't feel ignored myself, so why did she? Interrupting the work for such nonsense. It was as if her Suriname boyfriend had left her behind halfway through orgasm.

The bleating kept going. Resulting in: 1) a warning report because I blew on the bureaucrat-mouth whistle just for fun, 2) a warning report because I thought it was too crowded in the wagons to check the tickets, 3) a memo because I had filled an overtime claim form for immigrant consultation which later turned out not to fall within the definition of that consultation, 4) a memo because Waalders didn't want to go 'on code' because she was afraid to be harassed by me, 5) a memo because I had allegedly pardoned a mentally retarded man.

Whenever we went 'on code', before we started she used to shout that I was going to harass her. The shift supervisor came rushing in and said: "This case is over. You have to do this." She claimed that there was someone else who thought the same way, but no one had reported anything. Oh, what stupidity. There were rumors that Yvonne Waalders was caught with legs widely spread on a car hood near the metro station, and also about her fucking in the underground rooms of the metro station Weesperplein. We have been there once, but couldn't find any trace. They were too smart to leave any. Having sexual harassment 'on code'? Well, no. And with Yvonne? It would be a failed attempt. Well, at least she tried.

I had done everything that was possible to help resolving the tense situation that lasted too long, but I couldn't leave that job because of some clumsy people. Therefore, I contacted a number of professionals within the company. Without any results. It began to look like unwanted intimacy, so I did a request to the confidante in order to investigate what exactly was going on. The whole thing now reflected more and more in my performance evaluation report. I was portrayed as someone who couldn't get along with people.

In March 1989 I had a conversation—in advance to evaluation in May. In the report, all the incidents could be found. It was too much vague to me. I put my signature on the concerned performance evaluation report as 'for seen'. However, they gave another interpretation to it. The sector chief, Jan Groen, wrote later in a letter that it was incomprehensible to him that I—a law student nonetheless—could sign a report 'for approval' without any thought or reading. Presumably I had to leave the form unsigned as if I had never seen it. He forgot that we had mainly discussed the causes during the conversation, rather than the facts. "It's clear that we have to work on the causes. But, that's what was written and that's what it was all about. The facts remain" was the position of mister Green afterwards.

The next performance evaluation would be somewhere in October and was crucial for my permanent appointment at the municipal public transport service in Amsterdam. It was about my occupation, my livelihood. I had to make sure that it was not taken away from me. However, as the situation was, it was unlikely that I would get a better evaluation.

Since the Immigrants Consultation Board was there to represent the interests of ethnic minorities, I went there. But things got even worse. A meeting was organized. It was agreed that the Chairman of the Ethnic Minorities Consultative Metro would be present as an observer. First, an explanation was given about the circumstances that had led the evaluation committee to mark my score as 'does not meet the requirements yet'. The complaints of colleagues were extensively discussed. The so-called observation notes suddenly turned out not to be of importance any longer. They became 'snapshots in practice' and didn't have enough weight to influence the final evaluation. The one who made this formulation was my 'old friend' Ton, the staff advisor-annex-selector of the metro. For the evaluation committee it was strange that I had made an objection against the content of the evaluation only in the second instance, while I had already signed 'agree' before. Whether I had signed as 'for seen' or 'agree' did not matter to them. The point was that signing for 'agree' had apparently become the only option. The final conclusion was that the rating in the performance evaluation report wouldn't be altered. I had a week to submit a written, validly reasoned objection.

5. ARGUMENTS AND SIGNALS

The next day I went to the office of the Immigrant Consultation Board in the Scheepvaarthuis to look for help. The office was next to that of the Central Representative Committee and was not far away from the confidante. It wasn't the task of the confidante to interfere in this kind of labor conflicts, so I hadn't involved her in the case about the evaluation. Moreover, she was already processing an earlier complaint that still needed to be investigated. I was expected at the office of the Immigrant Consultative where the coordinator—Clay Voorland—was waiting for me. He was a man of Antillean origin who had worked at the GVB for years—Ton's former colleague driver. I told him what was going on and showed him some letters. He became furious. He grabbed the phone and called the chief Cabin Supervisors; Jan Groen. It was a heavy altercation by phone. He told the chief that the time for racism and discrimination was over: "It's finished. Basta!" I didn't know what I was hearing.

I had been in the Netherlands for a relatively short time, so all those oddities were new and unknown to me. At first I thought these people were joking. As usual, I walked around with a big smile on my face without any awareness that some years before a murder was committed because of racism and discrimination. It was a 15-year-old Antillean boy; Kerwin Duinmeijer. On August 20, 1983, in Amsterdam, he was stabbed to death by a 16-year-old Amsterdammer—a Dutch skinhead; a problem child who had grown up in a family that was facing difficulties, partly caused by the traumas that his Jewish father had sustained when his family was taken away—on the Waterloo Area in 1943—during the Second World War. For this reason, according to the judge, there wasn't enough evidence to define it as an act of racism. The judge deemed that is wasn't proven that he had premeditated his murder of Duinmeijer. Though still a bone of contention, it has been generally accepted that racism played a major role in this murder.

The conversation between Clay and the chief Cabin Supervisors struck like a bomb. The longtime hidden anger burst out and the advance of the Municipal Immigrant Consultation Board (GOA) began. An immigrant policy stemmed from a report by the Scientific Council for Government Policy (Wetenschappelijke Raad voor het Regeringsbeleid) of May 9, 1979 (*Allochtonenbeleid. [Immigrant Policy.]* Rep. 's-Gravenhage: SDU Uitgeverij, 1989). In the beginning it was called the 'anti-racism initiative'—an informal immigrants consultative group. The name was changed to Municipal Immigrant Consultation Board when it received formal advisory powers in 1989 and was included in the Civil Servants Regulation Amsterdam.

With that same furor Clay put together a letter on my behalf: an appeal against the performance evaluation rating. The letter was full of terms like 'I protest emphatically', 'I impugn' and 'I demand'. I signed the letter. I had nothing to lose anyway. The subway management, however, did not accept this objection. I was told that I had to write the letter with my own hands. And so I did it!

The letter was discussed on July 25, 1989. A member of the Central Representative Committee assisted me, a white man, but more than the statement 'in this organization, they can make and break you', he had nothing else to say. Because of this procedure, it became all the more clear to me that my suspicions were right: they were singling me out. There was indeed a certain discrimination going on and the leadership somehow wanted to make me—the victim of that discrimination—into a scapegoat. But then again, how do you prove this?

The evaluators did take note, however, 'that something was going on'. Had they been really objective, they would not only have talked about the facts, but also about their causes. But they didn't. That was a pity. Because we all actually knew what was going on, but we couldn't agree on what to do against it. By denial and concealment it would not be solved, and certainly not by appointing me as the scapegoat. According to the management we couldn't come to a solution because I 'didn't understand the problems entirely to the cause'. Was it so deep within me that I couldn't understand myself? Or was there a profound and entrenched problem of racism and discrimination and could the management itself not believe it? It was premature, according the management to mention the problem by its name.

The leadership assured me that they would take the arguments and signals very seriously. However, in the end all of the conversations, including those within the group, put no grist to the mill. The fact that the management itself led the procedure didn't help either. Whenever there were valid arguments on my side, they suddenly had a 'lesser degree of attention'. More than once the management had been informed about the course of affairs, including by Maureen Vreede, but the evaluators continuously pointed out that the given examples were merely signs of a 'relationship conflict' that was about to get out of hand.

In the end, the management of the GVB finally recognized the reality of the situation,—albeit with some reluctance. The people at the Scheepvaarthuis must have asked themselves: who wants to stand accused of racism and discrimination? To prevent discrimination charges, there was nothing left to do for the leadership of the GVB than to come up with an appropriate solution as soon as possible. Several chefs and the chief Cabin Supervisors were going on a vacation, so for the time being I was entrusted with station services only. In that way they hoped to avoid escalation. Off the record, a chief told me that it was very difficult 'to turn a large group of people around'. With that statement, I could taste the plan. How could it be possible that a large group just turned against me? Even people with whom I had nothing to do, like this man who appeared out of nowhere at the station and asked for my agenda. He had heard that I kept notes in a diary. And another one—accompanied by a chief—came along with a piece of paper in his hand and started screaming "That nigga did it." He had probably received a fine for traveling without a valid ticket or without the correct ticket and came looking for tha nigga. But which one gave him the flame?

Meanwhile, there was difference of opinion about the interpretation of the results of investigations. With more and more emphasis it was stated that there was a 'severely impaired employment relation' at work. The negative opinions about me remained unchanged; the evaluators maintained their taken conclusion. For this reason, I continued to challenge that performance evaluation. Early in July, I had notified the team leader and the chief VIC that despite all the conversations in and with members of the team the problems continued to aggravate. My colleagues incited each other to 'block' me and new colleagues were tipped about this 'blockade' on their first day. One of those newcomers was heard as a witness by the committee. He shouldn't have interfered with the affair, he was told. Another one found it all too much and informed the confidante that during a sick-call to him, the shift supervisor and colleague Verdam only spoke about the so-called problems caused by Anthony. The team leader even claimed to have confidential information about me that could possibly be used in the case. However, another colleague wrote a statement saying that there was nothing wrong with my attitude at the subway or my way of approaching passengers. She even dared to question the actions of some of her colleagues.

The problems were not only limited to the workplace. Verdam was arrogant enough once to come and wait at the door of my house early in the morning. I was shocked. He said that he wanted to go to work together. It was strange. We both lived in Bijlmermeer, but there was a considerable distance. At work I spoke about the event to a colleague. The story spread like a wildfire. People started claiming that Verdam had spent an entire night with me. Great nonsense of course, but the result of this gossip was a disruption of the peace and quiet at work, all for a taste of sensationalism.

I didn't care about that. It only confirmed once again that I had had enough reasons to contact the confidante earlier. She was well informed about everything and yet there still was an escalation. I didn't like that groundless rumor at all. Gossip has a function, but this was something else entirely. This was evil gossip aimed at deliberately damaging my reputation without any facts to support the rumors. Gossip—just for 'fun'—to avoid work (Dutch expression 'er de kantjes vanaf lopen'). It was a form of informal social control which I didn't ask for. For that reason, a few days before the new evaluation review of July 25, I had again caught up with the Confidential Committee; this time with an official complaint.

6. NOTHING SEEN, NOTHING HEARD

I had submitted the complaint at the right moment. The last performance evaluation—which would determine my appointment at the municipality of Amsterdam—was upcoming and the present circumstances could only have had a negative impact on the outcome. The battle for righteousness began.

Because of the vacation leave of the president of the committee, it wouldn't be until August before the Committee could deal with my complaint. The Committee needed more accurate information, however: about who had used which words and / or gestures on which dates, and about the witnesses. The confidante supported my complaint about discrimination based on my 'perceived' sexual orientation. Besides that, she knew a few things that she wanted to explain face-to-face. However, she would be absent until the end of August as well because of her vacation, as the chairman of the committee informed me. He asked if I wanted to wait for her, or if I wanted to talk to him first. I didn't see any evil in doing this, so I did talk to that man. The confidante hadn't told me that she was going on a vacation, so I didn't know if she wanted me to wait or not. I hadn't heard anything from her.

When she came back, I told her about my conversation with the president. She was furious and said that I was arranging things behind her back and that I was using her. It would have been better if she had sent me a note or at least given me a call to say that she would be away for a couple of days, but she didn't and she also had the nerve to be

28

loudmouthed about it. Well, fine then!

Meanwhile, I left the Immigrants Consulting for what it was. It couldn't help me. The office began to fill up with foreigners who thought they could cash in on my case. Furthermore, they wanted to do efforts only for highly educated black people. However, in the meanwhile Clay Foreland was eager to meddle in my complaint. In addition, the risk was not insignificant that others might misuse my situation in their own interests. Someone in the management said to me: "Watch out that the confidante isn't going to use you for her own benefit." Such a statement wasn't strange. After all, she was appointed to determine whether there might be racism and discrimination inside the GVB and, however strange it may sound, it was in her interest if she could prove that it was indeed the case. Nevertheless, she had probably not anticipated that she would get such a cross-border case.

Throughout the period that I was bullied and harassed, I have not seen or heard a single immigrant who had the guts to tell his indigenous colleagues that what they were doing was wrong. They all kept their mouths shut. They knew nothing. There were two Antillean VIC'ers who had sided with their Dutch female colleagues. "It was an anthill; you'd better stay away." one of them said to me. Who could know better? In Papiamento we have a saying. "If the shrimp tells you the mud stinks, believe it" (Si cabaron bisabo cu e lodo ta hole stinki, ker'e). Apparently no one realized how sensitive this issue was to me. It cut deeply into my private life. So deeply, that I didn't even dare to talk about it outside the GVB. It was new to me, I didn't know how to deal with it: a group of pushy strangers desperately trying to get access to my private life. Especially the accusation that I looked down upon my colleagues because of my high education struck me. Nevertheless, my job was more important to me than the abuses of a few colleagues who wanted to amuse themselves with me. With comments like 'I have a Turkish friend' or 'My neighbor is a Moroccan' or 'In another district they have a white gay guy', I could not buy bread.

As the day of the meeting with the confidential committee came closer, tensions rose. The confidante told me that she was threatened and that her phone functioned in a strange way. There had also been an attempt to break into her office: room 52, as her office was named. Just mention it, the cackling began again. My file was there well stored in a safe, so if it would disappear then someone must have known the combination, or one would have to take the whole safe. The confidante told me that she had been asked by the management to ask me 'what I really wanted' and if I had any plans. I found it very strange, because they could easily imagine the answer: I just wanted a good job and not to be harassed.

At the end of August 1989 the confidential committee accepted my complaint against the behavior of shift supervisor De Beer and colleagues Verdam and Ferrier. The accused Verdam and two witnesses were invited to be present. On October 3 the investigation would continue. The same person of the Central Representative Committee—who had also assisted me on July 25, 1989— was now the advisor of Verdam. Funny, isn't? The first substantive session was on December 15. It felt like I was on trial in a court. It was horrible. A contradiction to my impression in the West about Dutch people. A disappointment beyond the friendly Dutch smile.

In the meanwhile the date of my performance evaluation came closer. I had already given up hope for a permanent appointment. The situation had deteriorated rather than improved and the people who had to do the evaluation had turned against me. Karel van Zwol, the boyfriend of Inge van Daalen, got—as I heard later—a request to keep an eye on me. After the judgment of the confidential committee he asked team leader De Beer whether he still had to keep going. It was that underground, subcutaneous subtlety that the committee had so much trouble proving. "How do you do that?" the president asked to Verdam. He received the advice not to answer.

Just one day before the confidence commission's decision—which was not unanimous—I would have the last evaluation. The result was as expected. The Head of Human Resources, Mr. Schultz, was there too, but everything depended on the evaluator. He had the power. Schultz informed Jan Groen, the evaluator, about the fact that there was a complaint from me. He wasn't informed about it. "When did he do it?" he asked. "A couple of month ago." was the answer. Groen became red with anger. He crossed a few words on the assessment form so hard that he poked through a hole in the paper. I was shocked, I must say. I was shocked because the man was so furious, but also because it had now been confirmed that I was not eligible for a permanent appointment. The decision came a few days later and had a considerable impact.

What now?

7. THE GROUP STANDARDS

On October 17 the confidential committee decreed the following ruling:

"The Commission has established—among others things—that the damaged relationship in particular is related to:

a) the striking and / or feminine manner in which Mr A. would move and behave during the ticket control.

b) that Mr. A., in case of problems between colleagues and travelers (code 100), would not—at least not sufficiently—provide assistance to colleagues.

Some colleagues of Mr. A. consider the causes mentioned under a and b to be disruptive to their performance and think that he should change his behavior. The team chief believes that he needs to change his attitude and to try to understand the mindset of his colleagues. The Commission wasn't able to determine the truth of the allegations under a and b about the conduct of Mr. A. However, the Commission takes note that Mr. A. does differ in some ways from his colleagues. He has a more non-violent attitude towards conflicts with passengers, he is black, has a way of behaving that is reminiscent of gay men, and refuses to give his colleagues full disclosure about private matters. Because of this distinction, he apparently doesn't comply with the group's standards. His reaction to that is not smooth, due to which the relations are permanently disrupted. The Commission has also established that in the disturbed relation, colleagues treat Mr A.

unfavorably inter alia by means of 'wisecracks', whispering and ignoring."

One thing was missing from the ruling; the gossip. I was said to be a drug addict 'because I was living in the Bijlmer, I was black and all blacks are of the same kind'. It was a living prejudice. Many Dutch people agreed that the Bijlmer was the first and only Dutch ghetto. Being compared to the Bijlmer was the worst reputation a neighborhood could earn in Holland. The current chief of police of Bijlmer district, Ad Smit, even went as far as calling the Bijlmer a 'national disaster area'. [Sterk, B. and Zahirovic, S. (2015). The Bijlmer: a Dutch Approach to Multiculturalism by Boudewijn Sterk, Selma Zahirovic | Humanity in Action. [online] Humanity In Action.]

The committee didn't consider as proven the complaint against De Beer, Verdam and Ferrier, but it was not their intention to address anybody. If that were the case, then the whole GVB had to be tackled. The defendants consisted of a group of VIC's and the team leader. According to the confidential committee, he was not sufficiently above the parties. The committee advised the management to entrust the district manager at the Metro with respect to the VIC sector to adjust the group norms, to seek for a solution to the strained relations, and to report about the advances to the management.

As the facts were, I would lose my job on January 1, 1990. So I had to act quickly. Mr. Schultz, head of personnel Metro, sent me to the Central Representative Committee. There I was again and to speak to Bernard Kuyt. Once I was sitting with him at the table he picked up the phone and called someone. 'He's with me and can't go anywhere'. At his reaction, I could see that he had a not so pleasant answer. He asked me: "What's the problem?" I told him my story. A secretary joined the conversation to score it in stenographic. "We will immediately make objection at the Appeal Committee Cabin Stewards." Kuyt said. He wrote the letter and I signed it. It said, among other things:

"I want to make an objection to this second evaluation. I would like to give a verbal clarification about the points on which the assessment scores are negative. In my opinion, these points are related to the fact that I have complained to the Confidential Committee. This complaint has already been examined and is awaiting a ruling. So I hereby sign an appeal against that assessment; it is unclear to me whether this assessment will affect my appointment at the GVB."

Kuyt was one of the veterans who—through consultative bodies and committees—managed to get me an interesting position within the company. Tram and bus drivers who had known each other for years formed the consultative bodies for employees and I had to knock on their door. Meanwhile, I went 'into hiding' in the Illness Act. but on October 25 the company's doctor Bisschops intervened. He wrote a letter to the management of the metro, in which he stated:

"The employment relationship is absolutely, durably disturbed. Based on absence and performance, dismissal is inevitable. Considering the social and situational considerations, it may be right to immediately transfer him to a totally different district. There he will have to begin with a 'clean slate' ... to be absolutely clear, this is NOT a medical issue or problem. This is evidently a company management issue. Problems at work can't be resolved at home but only at the origin, namely at work. For this reason, the person concerned is declared by the BGD (company health service) to be fully fit for work. This degree will only be realized, however, AFTER a conversation with his direct supervisor AND end boss."

When I later visited the company, Bisschops put my medical file on the table. I noticed that there was something written with a thick red pen on the cover: "REJECTED VIC".

Me to the doctor: "What is the meaning of that?"

He: "Probably Peter stung a wet finger in the air."

It was another surprise from Peter, the medical examiner with his crystal ball. At that moment I actually didn't know what I saw and what to do with it. In astonishment, I kept thinking. "Can't you wipe it off with Tipp-Ex?" I asked him. Bisschops took a small jar and smeared the white stuff across the words on the cover of the file. Still, the evil had already been done. In fact, this smacked to forgery in employment committed by a public servant. Which—based on the law—is punishable.

From the beginning, I had had a feeling that there was something wrong with my file. Ton had already said something to me once about the medical examiner and now I had seen it with my own eyes. Peter had tempered with my file. Suddenly I remembered that I had applied for the position of metro driver / station officer in July 1988 and that I was rejected by the district manager Metro because I 'didn't meet the requirement of a high degree of employability for a longer period'. This medical file had probably been the reason. That mysterious fumbling surrounding the file later led me to file a complaint against Dr. Bisschops at the Commission of Physicians. I should have filed the complaint against Peter—the transvestite—however. "He wants to get someone." one of the members of the committee said. These people abused their position and the facilities they had at their disposal to send around hostile messages about me. Thus more and more people within the Municipality became involved; even beyond. In which manner? This comes later. In itself, I had never had a discussion with Dr. Bisschops. Perhaps that was the reason why he showed me the cover of the file. Or perhaps his conscience nagged at him? I have never seen the file again.

Another strange thing that happened afterwards was that the Central Representative Committee (CRC) told me that I had wrongly filed my complaint against the Appeals Cabin Stewards. According to the CRC, I was not, in fact, employed at the GVB, but at the Municipality of Amsterdam, so I had to be at the civil servant union, the AbvaKabo. A consultant in that office wrote an appeal on behalf of the union. This should have been the end of my dealings with the CRC and, with that, of my dealings with Bernard Kuyt, or so I thought. Little did I know that it was only the beginning.

On October 24 the management board discussed the decision of the Confidential Committee and came to this conclusion: "The board conforms to the decision of the Confidential Committee. The Personnel and Training Chief will be invited to contact the district manager Metro in order to investigate a solution to the strained relations and to report this to the board management." The confidante didn't agree with the decision of the Confidential Committee. We told this to the Executive Board on November 8, with the announcement that we would consider a request for revision. Moreover, the Confidence Commission was not unanimous. One member didn't sign the decision. She—a black woman of the Vrije Universiteit—had packed her things and left to Suriname. We would, however, await the decision of the management about my objection to the negative performance evaluation before requesting a revision.

Vreede, the confidante, told Kuyt that I was set for one year on a temporary basis at the district Havenstraat. He called me with the good news and asked me to come immediately to the Scheepvaarthuis, because there were some formalities to be done. This happened on 29 November. Contrary to what the CRC had previously said to me, I received a message that week from the Appeals Cabin Stewards that my complaint was accepted. I was given the opportunity to explain my case orally on Tuesday, December 5, but that was all superfluous, I had heard, because an agreement at high level had been reached. The performance evaluation was destroyed. However, there appeared to be one condition: I had to withdraw all my objections. I didn't have problem with that. I was basically offered a permanent appointment. That was the most important thing.

Meanwhile, I began to realize that the people at the GVB—who called themselves 'helpers'—became reluctant. After all, the GVB was their employer and there had been a decision at a high level. It was an internal matter which had to be resolved internally, but these helpers begrudged each other. The participation committee saw Immigrants Consultative Board as a threat, a club of blacks, and the Immigrants Consultative Board considered the Central Representative Committee as a club of white supremacists. The confidante dangled just about in between. For the Immigrants Consultative Board she was a good asset because she could have information that would strengthen their position. To others she was a pain in the butt. "Racism and discrimination inside the GVB? Come on, that kind of thing doesn't happen here." An often-used excuse. But by now we know so much better.

8. A NEW OPPORTUNITY

As of December 16, 1989, I was transferred to the district Havenstraat. It was a decision of the management at the head office of the Scheepvaarthuis. A number of arrangements had been made. Because of the difficult period that I had had at the metro, I would immediately start with my training as tram driver. Only the file at the Human Resources department would go to Havenstraat. In total there were four files: one for the Personnel Department, one at the confidante, a medical file and one in the office at Weesperplein. In the Scheepvaarthuis they had the confidence that the case was resolved. However, in defiance of the agreements made, some of the files that had been in the office atWeesperplein began to leak to Havenstraat. It would lead to even more mudslinging. I often say: "If you don't like something, don't look it up."

They were not happy with my transfer at Havenstraat. It was imposed upon them by superiors, or so they thought. They said that the Metro had to resolve its own problems and that they should not pass them on to Havenstraat. There we went again...

In defiance of the arrangements I was not placed in the driving training, but with the other tram cabin stewards. To me, it was a completely new and unknown neighborhood. The work was varied. Not just the metro direction Gein, or to Gaasperplas, but several trams and buses, which drove various routes. The advantage for me was that— despite the unpleasant circumstances—I could get to know large parts of Amsterdam.

On Thursday, December 28 an "inspection"—concerning to me—was carried out by Joost Moerenhout, the team leader. Everything was perfect, from dress and appearance to motivation. Yeah, the same story as at the metro. During the first week of January I would be told when my driver training would begin. That was, as I said, the oral arrangement, but it turned out that they preferred to keep me at the ticket control, so they could get to know me better. When I asked Wim Boelandt—in his position of head personnel department in Havenstraat—about the appointments that had been made, I got an arrogant answer. "Let them come." he said, "We are not forced to employ you here." He also seemed to be head of the department Transport. He didn't want to discuss the arrangements at all. It turned out that he had been awaiting a conversation with someone of the Human Resources department.

As for me, I couldn't wait and turned to the lawyer, LL.M. Nicolette Kloot. She sent a letter to Boelandt. He was not happy at all. "You said you found the work at Havenstraat enjoyable and now you are putting a lawyer on me!" was his reaction. That's when it became clear to me that they had filed documents about me in the Havenstraat that should have stayed at Weesperplein; under the ground, forever. It was not an official file only a collection of bits and pieces of shamble, but of course they did contain the way in which they had tackled me.

And then, early in February, there was yet another incident. I decided to give a passenger the opportunity to stamp his ticket inside the tram. This apparently was a reason for the whole team to stop working and to go back to the station for a talk. "Giving a passenger an opportunity to stamp on the tram just once cannot be a reason to interrupt the work for a meeting", Steef van Rijn, the head of the department Cabin Stewards in Havenstraat said at that meeting.

According to the shift leader there was more to it. The whole team had told him that I was not welcome anymore because of my behavior. As the confidante described it: "The metro blue print." During the conversation Van Rijn said to me that I had to realize very well that I was in temporary employment and that in the course of the year a performance evaluation would be made twice.

The strategies that they had taken over from the metro started to work. Whenever the group wanted to have a longer break, they just waited until I did some minor thing wrong that they could discuss. "We're going back" as they use to call it. At the metro, the same thing had happened. Sometimes, they deliberately provoked a conflict with a passenger. They could then remain hours pending to get the matter done and dusted, because the service Supporting Tasks had to get there and often the police as well. If there were no suspicious-looking passengers to catch, I was their main target. The whole group then went back to the station for a talk. I think they even had a code, because sometimes I could hear them whisper: 'U-code', which meant that something was about to happen.

It was not our task to check for fake ID's, but sometimes we were confronted with such cases. During the training, the instructor told us how to act. Personally, my opinion was that the detection of illegal immigrants in the Bijlmer was not part of the function of the VIC. We did not get paid for it. The only thing we had to do was check the validity of a ticket. To determine whether the individual had a valid identity document wasn't within our field of competence. If someone was traveling without a (valid) ticket and gave a name that the controller did not trust, he would just call the Supportive Tasks. They would do the rest. We only incidentally caught an illegal immigrant, but a crackdown on illegal immigrants in the Bijlmer wasn't our responsibility in any case. Besides, the violence that was sometimes used was beyond the pale! I was against such scenes. The instructions about this were very clear: "Be cautious, because someone may be watched by the police as well." Furthermore, establishing the person's identity was not easy. For example: an inspector once stopped a girl for questioning and asked her:

"What is your name?"

The child said: "Geengeld (NoMoney)."

The inspector wasn't satisfied with the answer. We entered station and used the phone directory for investigation. He dialed the number and got the answer device: "NoMoney family's speaking, good morning."

The inspector's head turned red.

Another example: a shift supervisor at Havenstraat was named Ed Vergeer, but I usually called him *Mister Ed*. It took him a long time before he figured out that I was calling him a talking horse. That poor man had experienced a hard time with this stuff. He couldn't make a choice on which side to be on.

My employment history was different from that of the fellow VIC'ers. Before I started working at the GVB, I had worked for a bigger employer; the Anglo-Dutch multinational oil and gas company. I was also active in a number of other areas; in particular the arts. The VIC'ers at metro and tram were mostly young people who had lived on benefits for year. The VIC project was to prepare them for a regular job in the labor market. They had to learn a lot to gain work experience and social skills. There was a big difference between the cognitive abilities. They call it overqualification.

The chief Cabin Stewards in Havenstraat—Steef van Rijn— asked me what he could do for me. I said that I would like to continue the conversation with the team, but in the presence of the confidante. He warned me about the risks of such a conversation. The team or certain members of it could form a closed block against me.

9. PASSED, BUT NOT YET

In mid-February the shift supervisor was with me during a service 'to observe'. He was almost on my back to have a good look over my shoulder. And guess what. From one moment to the next I suddenly did nothing right. I would even forget to check some travelers. More 'observations' followed, and things got worse. The company social worker, Karin Bearer, found that it was no longer a case of the confidante Maureen Vreede. She wanted to take it over herself. "Maureen sees discrimination in everything." I heard her say. So they had already had a talk. In a memo dated April 10, 1990, Bearer wrote to me:

"With Ms. Vreede I have agreed that she keeps in touch with you about your 'future'. I understand that you want to go to the tram and this is promised to you. She will monitor it. Good luck."

After the performance evaluation in May 1990 I had had enough. I took a brief look at the rating list and told the supervisor that it would have been better if he had sent the whole mess right to the Scheepvaarthuis (the headquarter). That's when I immediately could begin my driver training.

The team leader tried to explain to me that he was only following the orders. "I had to make as good an evaluation as possible." he said. And that applied to me only? This time, however,

I categorically refused to put my signature on the evaluation. Shortly thereafter I was called by the head of the department Cabin Stewards, Steef van Rijn. He tried to change my mind concerning that signature, but I stuck to my position.

Van Rijn then sent a memo to district manager Ed Stuurman, the Governor of the Caravan (remise Havenstraat). "I have" he wrote "requested again to Mr. Anthony to sign the evaluation. The attitude which he took makes it impossible for us to work together in a normal way. He only had one answer that he kept repeating after each question of us: "I refuse to sign anything." I believe that, by now, we have done everything we could and what one reasonably could and should expect of us. We therefore ask you to put an end to this impossible situation as soon as possible."

A few days later, the head personnel department in Havenstraat, Wim Boelandt, was on the move: "On Friday, June 1, 1990, I again urged to Mr. Anthony to sign the evaluation form." he said in a small report on the GVB management. "I have stressed to him the official remedies present in the ARA (Public Servant Regulation Amsterdam). Mr. Anthony has requested further time for reflection, after which he told to Mr. R. de Lange of the ticket control department on the same day that he wouldn't sign the form." Whatever they did, I kept refusing to sign that form, because I knew what I could expect.

My refusal to sign worked out positively for me. On June 5, 1990, I could start with the driving training. The theoretical lessons were given by different instructors. There were three of us in the classroom. A Surinamese girl, an Iraqi boy and me; truly multicultural. There was only one problem: the girl required too much time to understand something and the boy had linguistic difficulties. From one moment to the other a boy with a disabled arm appeared: Sander. He kept close to me and although he did not speak a single word, through his movements I could understand what he was trying to say; people with disabilities may also be discriminated against. Piet van Straten was my driving instructor on the tram. He was married to a Surinamese woman. He was an easygoing man who knew well how to deal with other people. Apparently, he had also enjoyed his job, because one day he brought each of us a jar of home pickled cucumbers in vinegar. However, one day he made a significant remark: "It is difficult" he said "when other people want you to do things that you do not support." In his final report about me he wrote that everything was good and sufficient. "Sir Anthony has devoted himself greatly to the field tram driving period" according Van Straten. "If he remains committed in this way, I expect him to complete his training with a positive result." And I did. I passed the training for both types of trams; the old model and the new one.

Gerard Swinkels of the personnel department in Havenstraat called me to the office and informed me about a notification from April 1990 directed at all immigrant employees. In the context of a municipal project that would end September / early October, I would start a course on 'broad career orientation' for immigrant GVB staff. The purpose of the course was to provide immigrant workers who had shown interest in another job the necessary knowledge and skills. As such, they were eligible for other jobs within the municipal organization and even beyond. The course would take six months. I thought it was a good idea to join it to acquire more knowledge and skills. Swinkels hesitated a bit. Two months after the closing date of the notification, the course was in fact already full. Still, I was invited for an interview in mid-August 1990. I heard that I might possibly be placed on a waiting list. Afterwards, however, they had changed their mind: I could start right away with the first group. The training was given by the Noord-Holland Bestuursacademie. The policy to 'catch up backlog for foreigners' (Immigrant Policy - 1979) had stirred up a lot of emotions. Once again, the main problem became evident: the language deficiency. On the course there was ample attention for this, but often all they could say was: "In our country we say so or so." It was a matter of 1) communication, 2) interpretation, 3) cultural differences, and 4) giving others the chance without begrudging each other. Late in September the training started and by that time I had nearly completed my driving lessons. The exam was on October 8 and I passed—as already mentioned—for the license of driving skills, part trams. A day later I received my performance appraisal. It stated that I had met the requirements and was 'eligible for tenure'. My job description changed to 'aspiring people carrier'.

Anyway, I was making progress. Peter's scribbles on my file were obviously inoperative. After all, it was discredited by the head of the company medical service himself. Moreover, everyone could see me walk around anywhere in perfect health; EVERYBODY. Therefore, they had to resort to a new strategy. For them it was a matter of their honor and their reputation. It became a matter of personal principle. They had to and they would—somehow—show that I wasn't be suitable for anything.

On October 19, when I was still in a period where a mentor guided my work, I was commissioned by Wim Boers, the chief tram drivers, for an additional check. The honor was to Jeroen Staring. He reported: "Arrived three minutes late at Central Station. Parked the tram in front of the stop, and checked everything at his own pace. Regularly takes turns too fast." No one had ever told me that I had to park a tram behind the stop and then quickly get out. Staring's advise was to keep a mentor with me for a longer time.

There were also a couple of other reports about me; written by colleagues who had caused major accidents themselves and who may have been traumatized. One of them was a certain Mr. Petlan; a black man who had something to report to the management immediately. It had started all over again. I had once again become an object of discussion about whom everyone had an opinion. They were supposed to talk about the discriminatory treatment at the GVB, not about me! But ignorance is also an art—the hypocrite— and it seemed that they just wanted to keep on saying: "See, I told you so!" at all costs. But in such a way as to enforce the rights of their prejudices? They really couldn't stop. There we went again...

Now it was Stuurman's (the regional manager) turn to speak again. His conclusion was that I had to go back to the driver training by November 5, and that the proposed permanent appointment would be changed to a temporary one. It was yet another disappointment on behalf of the GVB, although it was not just a simple one this time. We are still talking about Principles of good governance; the way that I had experienced it. Maybe my expectations were too much, but I got such a bad taste of the whole thing that it became disgusting to me. "I do not know whether I will ever be happy with this profession" I said once. Of course these words were used against me. Stuurman and personnel manager Boelandt expressed their amazement about this. After all, I had made the choice for driver training, right? That was true, but I only began to loathe the trams, the district and the whole GVB, the whole bunch of shamble, because I had repeatedly been accused of not doing anything right. The men knew the situation. They were just trying to fuck it up. At that time, Boelandt especially was strongly opposed to my transfer to the Havenstraat. "If he cannot do well at the metro, than neither can he do so here" he would have said. Why not? Did he have something to hide? Stuurman has resigned and became head of the department Transportation and District Manager as well. That way, he now had three caps to wear. Swinkels was hired as staff advisor.

On November 22, the chief tram drivers again sent an observer: Jeroen Staring. He was well known to me. His report was very negative. According to him, I had driven too hard, I had driven through a red light, I had driven past tram stops. The latter seemed to be not so uncommon. At one time, a stone was thrown through the window of a tram with the following note attached to it (published in the Pantograph June / July 1990 – edition remission Havenstraat):

"You bastards. The big bastard who last night (Sat. 00:00) didn't stop with line 16 at the Valeriuskunier/Lairessestraat should pay for this window. You must stop—asshole—if anybody is waiting at the stop with a raised hand. This is the 2nd time already, Typhus Carrier."

The message was delivered. But Staring had a message to deliver as well. His advice was to deprive me of my tram driving license.

10. A BUSY MONTH OF DECEMBER

Through a letter, dated November 26, 1990, the district manager Havenstraat informed me that—based on the assessment—I was not eligible for a permanent appointment. A strange twist, because in October, I was still eligible. The public authority—an ass—rescinded after a few weeks because of a representation based on a performance appraisal made about me. The letter was personally delivered to me at nine o'clock in the evening by Swinkels. He had two men with him in blue suit, from the department 'Supporting Tasks' (company police). He had called me a couple of hours before to ask if I could stay at home, because he had a letter for me. He couldn't say what it was about over the phone. When they came in, I was peeling potatoes. That's why I had put the letter on the table, intending to open it later, but since the three men kept on standing in the living room, it became clear to me that they wanted to see me open the letter. Jokingly I said, "I'm going to eat a sweet potato and a regular potato to see how they integrate." The remark was not much appreciated, but the three stooges understood that I would rather see them get out of my house. They did. A lot of nonsense was written in the letter. Among other things, I could understand that in the assessment on which my rejection was based, it also was stated that I was indeed eligible for tenure. That seemed obvious, but it was not apparent. So we are back to the same stalemate as before, with almost the same actors: Bernard Kuyt and Maureen Vreede, now with the leadership of the district Havenstraat. I could stay at home to wait and see what would happen. And all that in the busy month of December... Kuyt repeatedly mentioned the date January 1. I had the impression that it was very important to him. In all of his proposals that date played a role.

On December 4, 1990 the confidante sent her findings to the management of the GVB. She wrote:

"In Havenstraat (per December 16, 1989) Mr. Anthony has initially engaged in control duties, much against the agreements and despite the calls from the confidante with the district leadership. The situation (intolerance of fellow colleagues at the subway) repeated here. Through the coordinator Central Representative Committee and the confidante, the driver training was made possible through a special management assignment for Mr. Anthony. The training period and the exam went very well; the client had finally proven his ability. He was successful and could face a permanent appointment ...

Conclusion: However much we attempted to give Mr. Anthony a new chance, and without calling into doubt the expertise of mentors, I want to state that this is not about the driving skills of Mr. Anthony: Someone who constantly has to work under the pressure of homophobic and other abuses is in a precarious legal position. He is under stress and it breaks him up! Nevertheless, I agree with the position taken by the district leadership with respect to the conclusions they draw from this."

Vreede criticized the secret checks carried out by me. "Inspections that are not reported beforehand are out of the question!" she wrote.

Just before Christmas, on December 24, 1990, I had lodged a complaint through my lawyer, LL.M. Kloot, to the Tribunal in Amsterdam. Therein Kloot set out:

"Anthony received a temporary appointment as a probationary extension from January 1, 1990, to January 1, 1991. However, his function was changed to apprentice people carrier. Anthony changed jobs because he was being discriminated against by his colleagues because of his perceived sexual orientation and perhaps because of his skin color. With help of the confidante this change took place."

At the same time there was a request for an immediate provisional measure submitted to the President of the Civil Service Tribunal. My lawyer argued: "The decision, dated November 26, that the municipality now intends to terminate the appointment on January 1, 1991, will cause huge and irreparable damage to Anthony if he will not—by means of an injunction—have an opportunity to continue working at the municipal public transport service, implementing the pending appeal. Anthony therefore has an urgent interest in a provisional measure." Additionally she stated in this request:

"The disadvantage that Anthony will have—if the attacked decision is implemented—isn't in proportion to the interest of the other party-if the decision is immediately executed. Anthony will suffer great harm from this disadvantage. If the decision is implemented, Anthony will lose his job and his capacity as an official. He also will suffer financial loss."

After Christmas I told Bernard Kuyt that the issue had been entrusted in the hands of a lawyer and that a complaint had already been sent to the Tribunal. In a hurry he went to the deputy director of the GVB, John Tjon A Lep, to tell him about the move. I had seen him before during an action in connection with burglaries at metro stations. By some immigrants, he was highly acclaimed. He was said to be a man who had always been amenable to reason. Personally, I had no experience with him, but I assumed that I could trust him. Kuyt arranged a meeting with him. The conversation with Tjon A Lep was held on December 28 in his office. They were prepared and the plan was ready. Before we went to the Deputy, Kuyt picked someone up, Mr P. Wagenaar. Tjon A Lep came up with a written proposal:

"During a period of six months, Mr. Wagenaar shall search for a suitable job for you, both through the internal and the Municipal Mobility Office. For the duration of these six months, you will be offered an employment contract for a light administrative function, for which you will be paid about as much as your current salary, minus grid and other related surcharges. Mr. Wagenaar is entrusted with the task to present a suitable employment contract to you before January 1, 1991. For the sake of good order I hereby let you know that his obligation to find a suitable job within six months depends on your cooperation."

I thought: "What a fuck is this?" First a permanent appointment, then a temporary appointment again and now a civil contract for 6 months? Furthermore, this six month contract would only be signed on the condition that I would withdraw my complaint at the Tribunal. I would have been crazy to ask my lawyer to withdraw the complaint and the request at the Tribunal, just because I was offered a contract for six months. There was a fly in the ointment. With the contract of six months as desk officer C, they would be able to discharge me after six months; with empty hands. No way that I would sign up for that! In a letter dated January 3, 1991, my lawyer wrote to Tjon A Lep:

"Wrongly it is stated in this letter that—on last 28 December—the client and you agreed that ... the client, however, is willing to carry out the proposed work until the President and / or the Tribunal has decided on the requested provisional concerning the appeal. As you know, the client still aims at a permanent employment as an official, starting from January 1, 1991. So, in order to show (again) his good will, the client will cooperate with your proposal of last December 28, on the condition that he will maintain all of his rights. It seems reasonable to me that the client will not lose out financially, which he will in the case that your proposal is implemented."

All of this happened during a period when there was a lot of discussion going on at the GVB about the discrimination of ethnic minorities. But what about me? Was I a foreigner who could be neglected?

11. A DECISION

In anticipation of the decision of the President of the Civil Service Tribunal, I had been detached (parked) at the clothing warehouse Tollensstraat. The verdict came on January 11, 1991, and was ratified on 14 January. The President of the Tribunal considered, inter alia:

"Based on currently known data, it must be concluded that the defendant (the GVB) hasn't demonstrated at all that the applicant (WA) hadn't lived up to the expectations which defendant was asking and could reasonably ask. To that end, we first considered that the applicant has passed the proof of driving skills—part of trams of the Public Transport Amsterdam—on 8 October, after which he was appointed as a prospective tram driver. Furthermore, after his training period, on October 9, 1990, the applicant was examined again and the submitted performance appraisal shows that the applicant met the requirements in all respects. ... The applicant therefore has successfully completed his training for tram driver, while he was also positively assessed for that function, so apparently he had met the demands made of him. Subsequently, the applicant started to working as an aspiring tram driver.

On October 19, 1990, an employee of the defendant had been watching the applicant for several hours during his work. Following this observation, a memo had been drawn up, which led to a conversation on November 1, 1990. On that occasion, further agreements were made about retraining ... The currently known information hasn't shown that the agreements from November 1, 1990, have been implemented before the defendant came to the contested decision. ... It is therefore also not proven that the applicant, after November 1, 1990, had driven inattentively or unsafe again. ..."

Excuse me for interrupting the panegyric, but anyone can understand that it is highly unlikely that barely 10 days after I had passed cum laude, had fulfilled all expectations, demands and requirements, and received a permanent appointment, I suddenly started doing everything wrong. The president of the Civil Servant Tribunal stated that 'a starting tram driver cannot be expected to immediately fulfill the function in the best way possible.'

Regarding the dismissal decision, the authorized representative of the Municipality said in Court that the dismissal decision could not be maintained for various reasons, but that the leadership of the concerned municipal service sector was not willing to accept that conclusion. Therefore, it must be concluded that we can by no means exclude the possibility that in the main procedure the contested decision will be maintained. The President was of the opinion that the question whether the contested decision was be taken on behalf of the defendant could and would be left open. The president of the Civil Service Tribunal suspended the dismissal of November 26, 1990, and determined that the GVB from January 21, 1991, had to give me the opportunity to work as a prospective passenger carrier until the final, irrevocable decision has been made. In other words, as of January 1, 1991, I would get a permanent appointment as official at the municipality of Amsterdam.

The appointment letter arrived in February. The fixed-term contract of six months for the position of desk officer C hadn't been terminated in compliance with the specified stipulations. In March, the complaint was withdrawn—by me—at the Tribunal. A normal move, as it is customary that the final, irrevocable decision would not be different from the decision of the President of the Civil Service Tribunal. But Wim Roelandt felt attacked in his honor. It was, after all, a serious loss of face for the Bouncer of Havenstraat. "The judge did not say we have done it wrong." he said. "We had to do it differently." He probably gave a different interpretation to the suspension. Thus, it was questionable whether the final, irrevocable decision could stop the fury of the Municipality. Even if I would have continued the case, they would have started a new dismissal procedure in due time, I was sure. After all, the issue was now completely focused on the person: my person.

A couple of years after the dismissal round at the metro, the second dismissal round was started. This round was even meaner. In fact, there had been no difference in the manner of approach in Havenstraat and the methodology—the 'blueprint'—used at the metro, except that in Havenstraat they had gone even further. At the GVB—considering what the municipal lawyer had said in court—they had already anticipated the negative decision of the Tribunal. Therefore, they had already contacted a psychologist from the Scheepvaarthuis in December, in order to take a psychological test of me. This happened after a person to person conversation between the psychiatrist and me. The test was mostly about my intellectual and personal performance. In a confidential report about the examination the psychologist wrote, among other things:

"After all he has been through in various parts of the GVB, a new start outside the GVB will be refreshing for him, in our view. What is most important to him right now is to settle his matters—if need be under expert supervision—and to make decisions about his future ."

To be clear: I did not sit in a corner at home to wail and whine, or sway and stagger in a pub to process my misery. I had other activities as well, such as my artistic life and other pleasures in life. I absolutely wouldn't allow that filth in the GVB to ruin that too. On the contrary! For example, during the time that I worked at the metro, photos had been taken inside of my house which would be used during presentations to recruit new staff and at the first Game Without Borders—a holiday for the staff of the GVB—I was performing as a singer on the outdoor stage.

That afternoon I met Ruud Besson, a reporter from *De Telegraaf*. He was the master of ceremonies. I had brought a backing tape with me to let them know that I was there. "Do you come here to perform?" Besson asked. "Well," I said "I'm really just stopping by, but I sure do want to sing a song." He accompanied me to the sound engineer, past some pushy immigrants who wanted to jump on the stage as well. The sound engineer put the tape in the machine and next thing I knew I was singing on the outdoor stage. If you could only see the faces of those wannabes and wannatoos! After my unannounced performance, I walked around for a while. The last performer at the event was René Froger—at that time still an upcoming Dutch artist. Mr. Tjon A Lep stood beside the podium waiting for him to give him an autograph. "This man can also sing well," I heard someone say about me. He could have seen me as extra in a television series too.

I never could have expected, however, that these things would be questioned when considering whether or not I could work at the Municipality of Amsterdam. It was even included in the psychological test—while I thought this test was only for the purpose of finding me a suitable position, as I had been told. In the advisory report of the psychologist it was written, inter alia: "He regularly performs as a solo singer and occasionally as an actor. Choosing music and / or drama as his main source of income could therefore be an appropriate and fairly realistic possibility. However, should he choose to sing and act only as a hobby and an extra source of income, the following recommendations apply: functions that bring little psychological burdens with them and in which the possibility to perform solo and as freely as possible, are the most appropriate for him."

After that, a long list of recommended functions followed. Had they waited long enough, they would have added to that list: "This man can also write, because he has written a book and a promotion brochure. Such a function—after intensive training—is not excluded." The test showed that I was eligible for a range of occupations. That result was quite different from what they might have expected. Based on the advice, I could not be dumped into the WAO (Disability Pension) in any case, as was suggested before. That was partly due to a proposed government decision to intervene drastically in the way the WAO was abused. Moreover, the standpoint of the company doctor—Mr. Bisschops—was known: I was fully fit for work.

After the adjudication of the Civil Service Tribunal, I had to return to the rayon Havenstraat, where I could do some temporary work in the porter's lodge. In order to get some rest I first took a few days off. My life next my work had to go on, I thought. It could not be that one group of people or another could decide what I did in my spare time. People of a political party asked me to join them on their list for the forthcoming elections in the district council of Amsterdam Zuidoost. Although I was not that interested, I said yes. In accordance with the Amsterdam Civil Servants Regulations I asked for one extra day off per month due to political and democratic activities. I was granted that additional day off with no problems. Furthermore, I found that the rest was not GVB's business. That's why I did not use any other facilities.

It is needless to say that they absolutely did not want me back in Havenstraat, and certainly not on the tram. The setup was: Anthony away from the tram, Anthony away from the GVB, Anthony away from the municipality and if Anthony could leave Amsterdam and the Netherlands altogether, it would be much better. In spite of the decision of the Tribunal on January 21, I had to return everything: uniforms, administration, cash box, cap, handbag, sunglasses and the bureaucrat-mouth whistle. In late January, a pseudo retraining— a farce as the lawyer later called it—began on the tram. As I could have expected, no matter what I did, it wasn't good. After two weeks of driving around, at one time during the ride, the instructor furiously pulled the emergency brake. That bell made quite some noise. "We go back to the remission." he said. He was like my private driver. The head instructor reported to the district manager: "I therefore recommend you to stop the training." I continued to do the work in the position of desk officer C. According to Swinkels, a change of posting would not be possible. Really? The formal function remained aspiring people carrier.

12. A NOTE FROM THE DEPUTY

In order to implement the recommendation of the psychologist, numerous discussions were held with the head of the Human Resources Department. In the meanwhile all kinds of brochures for study centers were collected. It was evident that I would not return to the tram. The so-called retraining was a farce; something to keep me busy while they were trying to find other opportunities.

For me, it was like a sightseeing through Amsterdam with a private driver facilitated by one of the Dutch largest municipal public transport companies. Maureen Vreede tried to help me make the choices. Sometimes it seemed as if she was about to begin a new course. She was kind of a counselor to me, which had somewhat weakened her position as a confidante. At the same time I got the feeling that she wanted to extract my attention from what was really going on. She asked me once if they could get into direct contact with the lawyer, so that she and Tjon-A-Len could maintain contact on my behalf.

The rumor went round that in Havenstraat they were urgently looking for jurisprudence to bring down the ruling of the Tribunal, so they could fire me again. I felt like the direct object of a lengthy legal hassle, but also as the centerpiece, and soon perhaps as a martyr; a future statue that would once a year be decorated with flowers—killed by an overdose of desperation. "Yes, it was really bad, but what good would it be?" I wondered. I could feel the anger tossing and turning inside me. It was a powerless situation, but I didn't have any reason to be desperate. My salary was paid on time each month. Later on, long after the second round dismissal, I got an uncomfortable feeling, but I did not become desperate. It was about a cheap loan for civil servants that I had to pay off. In a letter dated April 26, 1991, to Swinkels of human resources in Havenstraat, the confidante wrote:

"Dear Gerard. As agreed, I would do some work in advance with respect to Mr. W. Anthony, regarding a program of his choice. Bill and I have finally decided to go ahead with the study centrum ASR. Bill has opted for the course of computer bookkeeping, followed by the practical certificate bookkeeping. It was not possible to join the basic bookkeeping course, as there was too much time between the start time and it would require Bill to take an almost impossible catch-up ... In September the PD— Practice Diploma Accounting—training begins. It is therefore important to register Bill as soon as possible."

We were already in May and Mr. Janmaat, coordinator of the study centrum, informed Swinkels in Havenstraat that I had to follow the basic bookkeeping course before I could start with the courses computer accounting and PD bookkeeping. Therefore, it was very important that I would start following the course basic accounting right away. The GVB had hired a private teacher and Bernard Kuyt reappeared on the scene. He came with a private contract between me and Tjon A Lep, saying as of April 1, 1991, to May 31, 1992, I would follow courses, training and education. All this would be fully paid by the GVB. But there was a catch, because that contract also stated:

"No reason whatsoever will be accepted for not following the agreed courses, training and education, other than through long illness confirmed by the company doctor. ... If Mr. Anthony has not been able, during the abovementioned period of one year, to acquire the necessary knowledge for performing in another position, a dismissal procedure based on unsuitability for the current position will be started."

They created new excuses for the dismissal and this time discriminatory behavior wouldn't be a hindering factor for the GVB. It would be myself. I saw the paper for the first time in room 52: Vreedes' office. Kuyt was also there. It led to an intense confrontation. "What are you doing?" I asked. "Do you want to wear me out? It has not even been five months ago that there was a proceeding against my previous dismissal and now you are starting again!" Kuyt raised his voice. "If you don't sign this," he said "I will immediately initiate a dismissal procedure. And don't you think you will be able to live off your benefits, because they will be going down."

And there I was. I looked at Vreede, hoping that she would support me, but it felt like I was looking at a dead man; she didn't move at all. She was probably frightened by the hot reaction from Kuyt as well. It remained silent for a moment. She pushed back her chair and looked at me. Of course their plans were ready. They were absolutely not cheerful. Apparently my comment about the Tribunal ruling had driven them into a corner. "Now you are depending on our goodwill" the confidante said "It will provoke outrage if you call your lawyer again. Ideally, we should just talk to her ourselves. Do you want to give us her phone number?" Kuyt's face and eyes spoke volumes, but they didn't get the number. I remember how Kuyt, after a conversation with Tjon A Lep, said to him: "Soon I will put a gun to your head." I did not know what I heard! A strange joke! But apparently a common language between them because he smiled. Kuyt was an eloquent driver who had settled into a consultative body. Whenever I was in the office with him, he called the executive secretary. He mumbled something to him but the answer was obviously always 'no'.

So I sat in the office of the confidante, in front of two people who for a long time had appeared to be the ones who were going to help me. One immigrant, the other native. A third immigrant, Tjon A Lep— meanwhile—sat in his office upstairs or was walking around to organize something. I started to lose confidence in them. The only thing I could do was call my lawyer. I informed her about the contract. It was in concept without a date. My lawyer could do nothing with it; at least she did not do anything with it. I felt defeated, tired and sad. Strange thoughts went through my head, such as: "Who could still cause psychological harm to me right now? For those people, with such practices, I'd better be careful." But they would be unable to break the feeling of confidence in myself. For that matter, I had already raised the necessary mental barricades. Because, after all, I already knew what I could expect. It had happened before; the last caper with the contract was a confirmation. My confidence in them was already affected.

Oh well, it was all so logical. With so many people within the GVB who had formed a block against me, the outcomes were predictable. All those people—that coterie—at the GVB had to keep going on— together: Vreede, Swinkels, Kuyt, Boelandt, Boers and so on. They wouldn't start bashing each other. All of them had a 'take it or leave it' mentality. The trams, buses and subways must continue to operate.

More than two times had I been in the office of Boers, the chief Driver Services, to talk to him. "Now we're talking your lawyer's language." he once said. Furthermore, he did not want to hear anything about my case: "The less I know, the safer I feel."

Since April 1991 'Tjon A Lep's paper' was flung from one fax device to the other within the GVB, and perhaps beyond, but at the end of May a decision had to be taken. Apparently it was not important enough to talk about during office hours. An appointment was made after five o'clock, at Havenstraat, where the contract was filed by Tjon A Lep. On that evening were present the disctrict manager Ed Stuurman, Bernard Kuyt on behalf of the central committee participation, the confidante—Maureen Vreede, who was representing Tjon A Lep and I. The document was placed on the table. I thought I was going blind. What was there? The signature of Tjon A Ten; the Deputy Director General himself. That letter suddenly had a lot more 'weight' than when I had talked about it with my lawyer. "Why did that man do something like that?" I wondered. But I could still resist. I could still say, "No, I won't sign this" but the threats that I had received in recent months were quite something. What would the consequences be if I would persist in my refusal to sign? The paper lay there, on a gleaming oak luxury table. I looked at Maureen, then at Kuyt. Everyone was silent. The confidante pushed back her chair and Kuyt put both fists on the table. Stuurman looked at both of them and said "So it's a status quo?"

And I? I was brought down on my knees; I singed. The case was settled. That psychological thriller was too much for me. There was an atmosphere of mixed emotions in the room. Vreede remained silent. A couple of weeks later the engineer, Mr. Ed Stuurman, resigned after 14 years of service. I went home feeling like I had been declared an outlaw. My gut feeling didn't deceive me, as would become apparent in the months that followed. In fact, I had signed for my own dismissal at the long term. They would only have to maneuver astutely in compiling the file and then await the day of execution.

My duty in the lodge of Havenstraat was adjusted to the days and hours of the private lessons. However, problems started arising again right away. A colleague in the early shift—who had to go home at eleven o'clock in the morning—had to wait for me 'till one o'clock, or later, in the afternoon one time. Of course they complained about these things. Another 'colleague' wanted to set up his own trade union because of the 'the allochthones (immigrants) were given a preferential treatment' and he once came to me 'just to solve the problem'. Same old song! Not everyone was so hostile, however. One tram driver had a person-to-person business activity. He tried to sell me a water bed. Everybody could place an order for anything and everything with him in the gatehouse. Another driver said to his colleagues: 'Leave the boy alone.' But he was an exception. For other colleagues, the message was clear: I had to get out of the gatehouse at Havenstraat.

The last day of private lessons was on July 4. I had to find another job very soon, otherwise I would not make it to the last classes. On June 4, Swinkels left me a note in the gatehouse: "Bill, I have arranged an interview for another job on Wednesday, 05/06/91 at 11:30 with PAZ." [PAZ = Department of Personnel and Labor Affairs]." "Finally a real job!" I thought. But no: it was again a 'mutation site'. This time at Work Preparation & Planning; commencing on 15 July. That was the third time in one year that the GVB displaced me to that kind of job, despite my successful exams. I got a few days of study leave; I could stay at home until after the last private lesson. "Keep it up, it's almost over" I thought. But once again I was too optimistic. A new complication arose. The GVB was able to arrange a private teacher, but a private Examination Commission was something else. I had followed all the lessons, but I couldn't do the exam. The season was closed, so I would have to wait for another year. But the deadline—set in the agreement with Tjon A Lep—would have expired in the meantime. Bernard Kuyt thought this would threw a spanner in the works. "He'll just go to the next course" he said in a commanding tone.

Meanwhile, at the Department of Work Preparation & Planning, the usual turmoil started to emerge again. Was I there to work, or was I simply dumped for a course? That question caused friction again. So much so that the psychologist came along one day to see what was going on. Luckily, it was vacation time and I could again go into hiding; away from those people, from July 31 to August 26. After that period, the never-ending journey from conversation to conversation continued, almost daily. On the letter from Study Centre ASR to Swinkels, dated to October 17, 1991, a comment was written by hand, indicating that the private teacher had disappeared without a trace. A report could therefore not be made up. The private teacher had already cashed his money and left. Probably he was somewhere on the beach enjoying a sunny, well-deserved vacation. The study centre only wanted to have his official declaration that I had done the basic course in bookkeeping, but they could not find him anywhere. Maybe they wanted to give me a certificate of participation or something. After all, taking the exam for the officially recognized diploma was no longer possible in that year.

Jan Maat—the coordinator of the study centre—advised me to start with computer accounting in February 1992 and to do my exam in June 1992. I started to hesitate somewhat. Was the man a qualified teacher, or just someone who was hired as fast as possible by the study centre in order to please a large customer, the GVB?

In any case, an examination to determine whether I had enough basic knowledge of accounting was suddenly no longer needed. They remained silent about it. Just like that, I could start with the course bookkeeping PD, which began in mid-September. It was against Jan Maat's advice. It was a difficult task. During the day I had a hard time dealing with my working environment, in the afternoon I came home pretty exhausted, and then a few hours later I had to go to my course. I was quenched. Externally, I tried to appear as excited as possible, but internally I was at the end of my tether. "If things continue like this, I will drop." I thought.

The chef of the Central Technical Department in the Tollenstraat wanted to help me. I could start working there; they would accept me, but the accounting course should be continued in my spare time. They needed people to work there; not people who were present for a while, and then left again. I saw the move to the CTD as a good opportunity to get rid of that agreement with Tjon A Lep. On November 15, I applied to the business office of the CTD, where Mr. Leuring of the Personnel Department and CTD's chief Carelse, received me. I had a good chat with the chief. Of course, we also talked about that immigrants hassle. Anyway, I was told that I could start there.

I told Swinkels at Havenstraat about this new development, and also that the Deputy Director's challenged letter had lost its validity, because the content would be no longer feasible. Neither I nor the GVB could fully implement its contents. He said: "I want to break open the contract and discuss it with people higher up the chain of command. Then I did something stupid. On Monday November 18, I reported to Kuyt that it looked like I had finally found a permanent workplace. I should not have done that, as I immediately realized. They tried to rip me off with that contract. He was furious. "Not at all" he said. "Return to Havenstraat immediately! The agreement will remain firmly in place!"

13. "MEDIATION"

After two days hanging of around in the Havenstraat, Swinkels said me, "Bill, go home and stay home until a solution is found." In a letter dated December 2, 1992, he confirmed this:

"Unfortunately, till now it has been impossible to find a suitable mutation site for you. Therefore, I see no other solution than to allow you not to appear at your working place until further notice. In other words, until further notice, you do not have to work and you can organize your time at own sole discretion."

During the following days, he called me a couple of times. The holidays were coming up, so he proposed a great opportunity to share thoughts in a cozy environment. We made an appointment on a Saturday night in the penthouse bar of the Hotel Okura, which offered a beautiful view of Amsterdam by night. However, the meeting did not really provide the solution that I was looking for. Gossip was going around in the Scheepvaarthuis that Swinkels was bisexual and that he preferred black guys. I—at least—did not feel that he wanted to come on to me. The canteen was a suitable place for gossip. The meeting point of the cabal was at the table. I saw Peter—with his crystal ball—also hanging around there. Apparently, he wanted to test my hearing. He was whistling a long note. He saw me and I saw him. That was my last time in the canteen.

The management and corporate secretary, as well as the CMC

Scheepvaarthuis, had probably found out how that network talk worked. Their joint Christmas message of 1992 was:

"The larding of that 'chit chat get-together', we would like however to offer you in convenient way."

The intention of that meeting with Swinkels in Okura remained a mystery to me. In fact, the entire hullabaloo about my appointment remained a mystery. We chatted a bit and had a drink in the penthouse of the hotel and then we went to a nearby snack bar to eat shoarma. "You can possibly claim the receipts as work meeting" I joked.

Kuyt and Vreede also called me now and then. Kuyt gave me his private phone number at home. Vreede was more reticent. "We just have to keep a finger on the pulse." she said. She found that, despite the hectic pace, I was too quiet and calm; and that worried her. For a moment I thought they may have been afraid that I would commit suicide. In fact I didn't give a damn what they were doing. I saw them as a puppet-show whose direction had become confused. It was not about discrimination anymore, but about prestige. And what was it all for? Because a well-dressed man tried to withhold a job at the municipality from me? To what extent the activities of the VIC's were related to that could not be proven. Although, it is conceivable that his way of interfering with me at the workplace would have been noticed by others.

The moral of this story is the totally inappropriate, specious and superior manner of interaction and communication for the sake of prestige and power. Respect for and protection of an individual's privacy was enshrined in the *Constitution of the Netherlands* as a result of massive protest movements in the sixties and its impact on political decisions had been disregarded. This book aims to show how subtle and 'underground' things like these take place. Anyway, I got what I initially wanted. I had managed to stay out of the dole queue. With that, I had fulfilled my legal obligation to provide autonomously in the necessary costs of living.

Within the company buzz and panic broke; 800 jobs would disappear. A reorganization was on its way. I had to think of what Swinkels had once said: "If they want to kick you out, they will do it in the context of a reorganization." And so it happened. A team of public servants charged with the abolition of the Service Laundry, Cleaning, Bath, and Bathing Establishments was brought in to make a clean up in the GVB. These public servants claimed to have a good reputation in relocating surplus staff. In one report, the team member Mrs. Gerda Schouten expressed it in this way:

"We have already retrained and transferred hundreds of men and women (especially unskilled workers belonging to many different ethnic groups) to (often higher) administrative functions."

On December 30, 1991, I had an appointment with Vreede and Kuyt in room 52. I was told that in the spring of 1992 I would be carried forward to the Mediation Team. A new "revolving door" construction. It was careless and disrespectful of the rules, but I could not refuse, because then I would not meet the obligation which was imposed on me by Tjon A Lep. Having been commissioned by Swinkels, I was still at home. Bernard Kuyt called me in the first week of January. "Guess what?" he said "You are sitting at home pocketing a salary while we are doing the work? Come to the Scheepvaarthuis immediately!" I had nothing to do at home anyway, so I went to the office straight away. For almost a year I had worked in that monumental building, equipped with a paternoster lift (Roux Combaluzier, 1928). Starting at the Utilization Rate Measurement Dept. and finished at General Service, the Department of Post and Archive.

It was already known that in time people would have to leave the department. The librarian—a Doctorandus (Dr.)—was fired and I could clean up the rest. The service library was gone as well. I had mixed feelings. On the one hand I had the feeling that I was subtly being reduced through an intermediary. On the other hand I got the feeling that if I really did my best I could possibly stay at this department. However, there were still too many people busy with me without achieving anything. And I did not have the energy to claim the right on a position. Moreover, what would I have to claim? I wasn't in the situation to claim anything. I did not have the proper status—and they knew it. Claiming a position was only possible for personnel that belonged to the so-called 'RAP'ers'. These were people who, due to restructuring, cutbacks or medical causes through no fault of their own had lost their positions at the Municipality. They could claim priority in getting a new job. That provision was not intended for someone who was bullied.

Meanwhile, I had worked for almost a full year at the General Service Department and was wondering if I could therefore claim a position. The Mediation Team had a different opinion about that. Rather than to support me for a permanent place at General Service, Gerda Schouten wanted to dig in my network of acquaintances. I was getting sick and tired from those unwanted interferences. When the team did not sufficiently succeed in its aim, they tried to shift the blame onto others. They would be squared up by them. No wonder, she was there to kick some people out and it was not going to be easy.

Sometimes one could smell that she had forgotten to take a shower. They themselves were in an insecure position as well. They had to scratch out their own job at the Laundry, Cleaning, Bath, and Bathing Establishments.

When my final dismissal came before the court—more on which later—Gerda Schouten wrote a declaration which stated among other things:

"In addition, my activities with Anthony were made difficult by the contacts he maintained within the GVB ... He had contacts with two people who had supported him in the first proceedings; false hope was given."

She also declared:

"The GVB made fls. 10.000,00 available for Mr. Anthony to attend training and courses ..."

I didn't know anything about that money and was therefore surprised to hear this in the court. Schouten also brought up my 'private business' in front of the judge. She was referring to my hobby as a singer and that I had been on TV. In 1992 I had produced a CD—'A Helping Hand'—entirely in my free time and without any financial support from the GVB. Did she really think that I would have isolated myself from everyone? If I had baked a cake, would she have told the judge as well? The little promotional booklet was all that was printed by the Repro department of the GVB, which was a provision that was open to all staff, so it was nothing special and certainly not an example of preferable treatment of an immigrant. The content was quite special.

That's what made the difference! In the attic of the Scheepvaarthuis, someone had a booking agency for artists; Jen de Boer. That was an excellently running private business at work. The agency organized the Jordan Festival. I myself had once performed at that festival, where I had sung 'Mi Lobi Amsterdam'. Jen de Boer also had to vacate his post.

Gerda Schouten's anger stemmed from the fact that I had refused to expose my network of acquaintances. I was asked to make a list of names of people I knew. With that list in hand, the Mediation Team would work to see if those people could do something for me, but I definitely did not want to make any list. According to her, my refusal had worked as a self-fulfilling prophecy; an ancient theme in the mythology of the Greek and Indian antiquity. Oh my god, an administrative entity which takes decisions based on self-fulfilling prophesy! I thought that only Peter had a crystal ball, but Gerda had one as well. Well, I told her that I did not believe in that nonsense. If it was up to the power of self-fulfilling prophecy, I would have become a millionaire long time ago. I still dream about that every day! But why should I issue my private directory of names and phone numbers to the municipality? To fulfill their prophecy?

"So plain is the mechanism of the self-fulfilling prophecy in these instances that only those forever devoted to the victory of sentiment over fact can take these specious evidences seriously. Yet the spurious evidence often creates a genuine belief. Self-hypnosis through one's own propaganda is a not infrequent phase of the self-fulfilling prophecy." [Merten, R.K. (1948). The self-fulfilling prophecy. Antioch Review, 8, 193-210.]

To satisfy the need, I had invented something and I noticed that they had sent out some letters: to John de Mol, the NOS, Radio Amsterdam, the 'Antilles House', some theaters, and private persons. Schouten: "Those letters were written by me, because he couldn't do it by himself. He only had to affix his signature." In dire situations, indifference and desperation can strike very hard. As a professional recruiter, writing and sending such mailing letters? Actually, I had to break off contact with that spyware, but because of her meddling in my personal things, I could use her very handily. I let her correct the text of my artistic brochure and made good use of the in-house printing from GVB to print thousands of it.

If it would have lasted longer, I would have demanded that a demo cassette—with my singing and bearing the logo of the municipality—had to be added. Yeah, the coat of arms of Amsterdam: 'Heldhaftig, Vastberaden, Barmhartig', meaning 'Valiant, Steadfast, Compassionate'. A few demo tapes were already recorded in a basement studio in Amsterdam. I was close, that a few boxes of my CDs—launched in October 1992—had already been sold to the GVB. As the confidante once said, I would have to squeeze every last drop out of it. Give a little, take a little. Right? For what, burps what! Sticking the face with politics in other people's life. A copy of the brochure—for which I had hitched Gerda to the cart—is preserved in the archives of the Dutch Pop Institute, the Memory of the Netherlands and the Special Collections of the University of Amsterdam. It's a great honor to be a included in the Special Collections of the University of Amsterdam.

As a beginning law student, I was a bit amazed that a public authority could penetrate so deeply into the private life of a citizen; even though I was a civil servant. I protested against , because in my inn there was no place for that kind of fuss. But in the treatment of my dismissal, the Tribunal interpreted my protest as an evasion of the 'duty of effort', which the Municipality had imposed on me to help me find a job. He said something along the lines of: "Well, it may or it may not have had the desired result, but the Municipality has at least done something."

At my departure from the Scheepvaarthuis, the company lawyer said to me that I could write a letter to the City Council and tell them what was going on. Previously, I had not thought much about it. Too much was going on at the same time. It was no longer clear to me. In August 1992 I left Scheepvaarthuis; I received an internship – for six months – in Zuidoost; my hometown. On the infrastructure Department I could take a place within the administration. I spoke about my appointment with Mr J. Degens of the city part and B. Schaapman of the GVB. My internship supervisor was Mr. Stevens. But here also there immediately were two downsides. To start, it was nothing more than an internship, at the bottom of the list of certainties in terms of work, and in addition, a reorganization was oncoming. A female council member or the political party CDA [Christian Democratic Appeal-Christian Democratic Appeal] said loudly that the borough had to focus on its own core tasks. The head of infrastructure came to tell me personally what the consequences would be.

I was there once again. My 'private business' really could have nothing to do with it. That I was faced with dismissal once again made me sad, because I had again passed a course successfully: the 'certificate spreadsheet' for bookkeeping. I had acquiesced at the inevitable course of events. My file was left at Havenstraat and became a target. Even two years after my departure, it was still loaded with reports, produced at the request for the preparation of my dismissal.

Then there appeared a new kid in the show. From the

Scheepvaarthuis a request was sent to Havenstraat to send a report about me. Mr. Prince, of the Department of Work Preparation & Planning, responded. "That man has left months ago. Only now you're asking for a report about him?" He got a tight reply back in the form of an assignment and messed something back way. Probably, my file was in the daily sight of Boelandt and it had to be filled up. I myself wasn't there anymore. I was out of their sight. It was a matter of time before my stuffed file would be sent to the Mayor for his signature regarding my dismissal, but on 23 april 1992 Wim Boelandt wrote me a letter:

"Given the opportunities and the positive expectations that Mrs. Schouten has expressed in respect of a possible relocation, I agree to extend the deadline, that you had agreed on with Mr Tjon A Lep concerning the termination of your employment."

Eh, eh, that was finally put on paper by someone. Boelandt asked for my cooperation "to bring this long-lingering case to a successful end." I found that somewhat strange and not very credible, because previously he had clearly let me know: "This requires us to terminate your employment effective immediately." There he had spoken his true intention., but now he had confirmed it.

I had finally ended up with an 'internship' without perspective in Zuidoost, because I had given cooperation to bring this long-lingering case to a successful ending. They had chosen the wrong path to get me to a suitable position, however. Back in December 1991 I had told this to Bernard Kuyt and Maureen Vreede, but they didn't want to listen to me. Kuyt did not even know what RAP stood for even though he was in a representative advisory commission. He wore a hearing aid so he probably never heard its meaning. Only the chirp! In such cases, they say: "He has heard the bell ringing but doesn't know where the clapper hangs." The position of tram driver would not eliminated, but apparently I had to leave anyway. "Then give me another position" I often said. The answer was always 'No'.

14. AND THEN FIRED

Finally, the file burst out. The expected dismissal with which they had threatened me for years was finally delivered on June 11, 1993. The relevant decision with the number 373/3 Capz 1993. Officially the news was that:

"Due to incompetence and / or ineptitude other than by reason of illness or disability, as of 14 August, 1993, resignation from municipality service was granted."

Thus I ended up in the Public Servants Redundancy Pay Scheme. But what was my other 'incompetence?' I wondered. My lawyer informed the GVB—too late, in my opinion—about the RAP scheme. Could it be used for me? On behalf of the GVB, LL.M.R. Woesthoff answered in November 1993: "To the category of RAP'ers belong (R) those who have lost their job due to a reorganization, (A) those who have been rejected and declared repositionable, and (P) those whose job has been canceled as a result of an austerity measure (P) (government cuts) ... Therefore, Mr. Anthony doesn't meet the RAP requirements ... These are exclusively reserved for the abovementioned categories of staff, who through no fault of their own have been fired."

I appealed to the Tribunal against this dismissal as well. My lawyer again asked for an injunction, so I could continue to work, but she also was thinking about challenging the judge. It would be the same judge as in the previous procedure in 1991. In his verdict on the injunction—passed on September 1, 1993—the acting President of the Civil Service Tribunal took note of the illustrious letter of Tjon A Lep. Once again it was proven what kind of vile trick—in fact—they had pulled on me. The judge stated: "Finally, it may not be entirely ignored that the applicant has been informed in March 1991 about the conclusion concerning his unsuitability for the job as a people-carrier, and he then agreed with that conclusion—the agreement signed with the Deputy-director of the GVB. The applicant did not provide any reservations and afterwards—during the mediation period specified— he had also never again indicated that he *would want to work as people carrier again*."

That was—with all due respect—a bullshit story of this judge, because by signing the note I had absolutely not consented to the conclusion that I was incapable of transporting passengers. They had put me under great pressure—which looked suspiciously much like blackmail—to agree with the study discipline that was imposed on me. Besides that, I did comment on that note later on; when I had a conversation with Tjon A Lep on January 14, about how Ms. Schouten had interceded, for example. I wrote him a letter about that agreement. Perhaps I didn't state it clearly enough, or did the letter have to be written by my lawyer? The mediators did not want to know anything about lawyers. That had become evident in a cold letter from Mrs. Schouten. Inter alia she wrote on July 15, 1993: "Furthermore you indicated that you would address letters and / or other communications from me to your person to your lawyer, Mrs. N. Kloot and that you wouldn't take up any contact with you."

Maybe the message had not come across clearly enough, I thought, so once again I went to the city hall in person to explain a few things verbally. Why would they bother me, knowing that nothing could be done. In fact, it made no sense; there was nothing more to save—not even by a lawyer. Meanwhile, the nitpicking continued. When I once called in sick, an instant message about this was sent to Havenstraat. They sent an inspector to check my condition and he / she made a wrong note. Result: I was summoned in the Havenstraat. They soon discovered the error, however, of which I was informed by telegram. It read:

"The appointment with J. Brandt on April 15, 1993, is canceled. There's no need to make a new appointment, because you have abided on April 8, 1993 by the regulatory measures for absenteeism."

Shortly before my dismissal would be treated by the judge, LL.M. Kloot stopped working as lawyer. She said that she wanted to be an interior designer. She carried my case to her confrere LL.M. R. van Diemen. The case that she had to submit to the court was no longer a simple discrimination issue that should have been firstly assessed by the public servants' judge. Since the GVB had done its job in that respect; it now was about something quite different, or so the representative of the municipality stated. The question was: had the municipality of Amsterdam and the GVB done enough to secure a new job for me? Simply put, they were splitting the case in order to get away from the discrimination issue. The beginning of all the misery—the discrimination—was ignored. It was a strategy that worked, because this time the Municipality won, before the same judge. In stating the grounds for the judgment, the magistrate said inter alia:

"In the previous procedure, a provision was made based on a decision of January 14, 1991, that stipulates that the plaintiff should be given the opportunity as of January 21 to carry out his duties as a prospective passenger carrier. But given the fact that *the deadline* had passed for a temporary assignment this could only happen through a permanent appointment. This had no adverse effect on the legal position of Mr Anthony."

That was true; for a short time. The magistrate further considered:

"The report of Ms. Schouten also shows that the defendant (City of Amsterdam) has made sufficient effort to provide the plaintiff with other work. To the plaintiff the opportunity has been given to attend various courses and the defendant has mediated in several applications ... That all of this did not lead to the claimant finding other work, however, is rather due *the disadvantage of the plaintiff* with respect to candidates with the so-called RAP status—who applied for the same job—then to the way in which the defendant has implemented the mediation efforts."

The Tribunal confirmed what I had already known for all these years and against which I had objected in numerous interviews: namely that mediation for me was useless because I did not meet the so-called RAP requirements.
Gerda Schouten knew that too, which is why she chose to dither around with my private contacts.

The judge wrote:

"The court therefore considers hereby that any lack of quality on behalf of the defendant's mediation cannot be blamed on defendant, since the plaintiff's formal position *was not equal* to that of a RAP'er."

Thus, Gerdas' self-fulfilling prophecy came true because of this unequal position. In short, it all had been a first class dry trumping up to kick out that nigga. For what? Did they begrudge me for receiving a monthly salary and benefits? As for the goal to get a job, they knew that mediation in that network actually would not have any result. In my point of view, the court might as well have come to the conclusion that the municipality had not examined carefully enough whether I could be placed in another position within the municipality and under which conditions; at least, they did not take the measures necessary to eliminate the inequality. There had never been a reassignment investigation. If they had done so, they could have determined whether I—while not being RAP'er—could for some other reasons be entitled to a priority claim. With this argument and in such a case, the municipality would again be the losing party. It would be the second loss of face for Boelandt cs (socio com). Should they then have risked a third round?

About the arguments submitted by GVB to justify my resignation, the judge said:

"According to the jurisprudence of the Central Council of Appeal (CRvB) the following is meant by the inability of a public servant for his job: not fitting in that position because of being endowed with qualities of character, mind or spirit. This functional incapacity must further also be derived from the actions or conduct of the official concerned."

I thought about what this would mean in my case. How was it possible that the same president of the public servant tribunal—who suspended the dismissal by order of January 11, 1991,—was taking into account my mental state? After the last verdict I had never worked as a tram driver. GVB had ignored it. In the four years prior to this new dismissal I had only done administrative work. No evaluation had ever been made. How could they have known about my perceived inability? From the same documents of the previous dismissal?

To me, the magistrate delivered a *panegyric* on my personal characteristics. Throughout a long time period following the decision of the President of the Tribunal, I kept on going and showing my true skills in different jobs. But strangely enough, it seemed that when enough people write pasquinades—whether true or not—about my 'character, mind or soul' and are supported in this by the leadership, then—according to the Central Council of Appeal [Centrale Raad van Beroep]—I would be screwed; my fate was sealed forever. Apparently, the judge began to understand that they didn't know when to stop. They just messed something together to give them their liking. By accusing me (or should I say praising me?) of being endowed with qualities of character, spirit or mind. At the same time, however, these people were evidently suffering from an obsession, since this was manifesting at all levels. In my opinion it was so widespread that you could call it; *the national tall poppies syndrome.*

In her plea my, lawyer had still insisted on that history, to include among others:

"After that permanent appointment Anthony has never been on the tram, so there was an employment contract under civil law (without a job) and there was a permanent appointment (also without a job). The GVB, however, was in trouble; it was in fact doubly bonded to Mr.

Anthony ... The plan was devised to establish the 50/50 agreement, apparently as a way out of this impossible situation. It was up to the counselors (Mr. Kuyt and Mrs. Vreede) to move Anthony to sign the declaration. Basically it seemed to be quite a good idea to Anthony. But because they had threatened with dismissal if he did not sign, he had immediately expressed his unease. He had to choke or swallow: Anthony chose to sign."

The lawyer said that the decision to dismiss me was—in the alternative—right based on the claim that mediation and training did not lead to another position. "But why had it failed?" she asked, pointing to a summary: "First of all because of the uncertainty about the legal position and status of Anthony. Subsequently, because of the construction of the 50/50-model. Finally, because of the difference of opinion on the mediation between the mediator (Gerda) and Mr. Anthony. This all point to one conclusion: the legal position and the status of Mr. Anthony were continually unclear. He did not appear to have the RAP status, while all the vacancies for which he could have had priority to apply, such requirements were needed ... He could not have prevailed when applying for these jobs.

The second point: the 50/50 concept that was chosen was gloomy, although it sounded good on paper. Mr. Anthony went from here to there; inside and outside; working here and working there; studying; mediation here, mediation there; interviews with Human Resources; interviews with counselors; late night phone calls at home from Personnel Department; in the evening in the bar of the Okura hotel, and all that did not get him a permanent job.

Point three: the difference of opinion between the mediator and Anthony. Ms. Schouten had a full, clear and precise mandate to mediate Mr. Anthony to anywhere, as long as it was not in the GVB or the Municipality. She began by writing to the theater and television world, much against the wishes of Mr. Anthony. Anthony had his reasons. Firstly, because he wanted to stay at the GVB; secondly, because he didn't want to utilize his hobby and private contacts in 'labor disputes'; and thirdly, because a job in that sector could not be achieved with cover letters."

In hindsight, it looked like a hilarious theater at Court. I sat there watching the spectacle and listening, but when the lawyer began to speak in metaphors I got confused. She used the word "aanfluiting" (mockery) and I thought she referred to the officer's flute I once blew on. She then passed the word to me. I could only tell the judge what the GVB had promised to me.

The judge asked me what I was doing.

"Applying for a job." I replied.

"Finally, just this." Mr. Van Diemen continued. "At the time of the first provisional relief in January 1991, the municipality already had to recognize and acknowledge that the GVB did not accept the court's decision. Even when your President decided against the municipality's interests, the GVB still did not feel challenged and it has remained that way. We cannot change anything about the internal relationships within the Municipality. The Board of Mayor and Aldermen of the City of Amsterdam, which is now again addressed, remain responsible."

The report of the Confidential Committee concerning the discrimination was not mentioned anymore. It had vanished like frost under the morning sun. In my view, this report should have had an important role in the dismissal issue. Only then a true and fair view of the relevant facts and circumstances could be constructed. The Municipality could, in the next phase, easily have come to another fair and reasonable solution, had they not been so focused on 'resignation, dismissal, screw him'.

Also, at this second dismissal trial my lawyer—as said—requested a preliminary injunction. The judge denied the request. The reasoning was as follows: "After the dispute about the permanent appointment, the applicant was aware of the criticism about his performance, so he knew he had to carry out his work as well as possible during the retraining." Of course I knew! But how could I have done my job properly when almost daily secret reports were made about me? I wasn't in the position to explain and contradict everything. The results were an ever thicker growing file about me and a case that grew, entirely unnecessarily, to a matter of prestige for the management of the GVB. As a result, the leadership even flat out refused to implement a court order. Besides, all of this was accompanied with such an abundance a projection of force! That was in my view not in proportion to the case concerned. A mob—mostly made up of men—could conspire to establish that the decision to dismiss me was based on a valid ground in law. What a shame!

The legal case about my second dismissal took place on Januari 23, 1995. During the years leading up to that date I was at home enjoying my redundancy pay. I monthly filled in the form and checkout. Every now and then a job was offered to me through the Municipal Mobility Centre, but that was it. That was when I got the uncomfortable feeling by realizing that something had really changed. The redundancy pay was gradually decreasing and was about to expire in December. Only a miracle could save me, but Mrs. Van Diemen called me with the bad news. The documents showed that they were all against me at the GVB. The procedural documents delivered by the Municipality consisted mostly of the reports from the dismissal procedure of 1990/1991. What

Gerda had to tell me, however, was new to me, and Princes printed it on demand. A certain Anima also wrote a note.

At the reconvened hearing I was assisted by LL.M. Van Diemen. The GVB was represented by a representative of the Municipality; the same LL.M. Woesthoff. Wim Boelandt and Gerda Schouten were there as witnesses against me. They were sitting all the way in the back of the hall. Gerda argued, among other things, that it was sometimes very difficult to communicate with me. What the hell?! Forcing me to share my private life because she wanted to? "Communicatively, it is very difficult to really get through to him" Schouten said "Some often do not know what he is thinking or saying. Sometimes he has strange ways of expressing himself, which are not understandable. Sometimes he expresses himself in certain ways of thinking, stopping in mid sentence. I have not yet discovered whether this happens consciously or not. I once talked to him about my experiences and my limited possibilities." She also told to the judge that her mediation work in 1991 was awarded the A&O fund prize (Stichting Arbeidsmarkt en Opleidingsfonds). My arsenal of prizes was not in the pleadings of my lawyer. It was evident to me that the mediator would experience a positive court ruling in my favor as a slap to the face.

When asked by the judge what the meaning of the employment contract was, Mr. Woesthoff didn't answer. Later on, I joked about this with the lawyer: "Actually, now I must receive two salaries from the municipality." She then said: "Keep your mouth shut. Don't do it."

On March 6, 1995, the judgment (case number: 93 AWB 611/612) was given. The GVB had been put in its right; the judge found my dismissal justified. When I heard it, I could not escape the impression that the judge simply had succumbed to pressure from GVB. Subsidiary the dismissal was admittedly justified—also according to my lawyer—but when taking into account all the circumstances, primarily my dismissal, it should have been nullified. In addition, I could also sense that the court actually wanted to protect me against the 'sickening atmosphere', whatever it was, at the GVB. He had probably seen deduced from my facial expressions, that I was pretty scared of what was going on. That comedy could have resulted in a bad ending for me in the snake pit. Now I could say it was all subcutaneous racism and discrimination, which was served with a wink; harassment purely for pleasure. It is incredible how people can live with this kind of hypocrisy.

Remarkable was also the reaction of the lawyer outside of the courtroom. She said to me: "They should had never employed you." So basically she was not 100% behind me. Much against her will, she had taken over the defense. This could be noticed from the moment of the first interview at her office. She said that she did not like *leftovers* from other lawyers, but preferred to start a case on her own. It didn't surprise me, because back then the thinking was 'no American-style' here; the US 'compensation culture'. An appeal could have been lodged at the Central Council of Appeal against the ruling of the Civil Servant Tribunal. There probably were reasons for appeal stated by the Tribunal; the unequal treatment, no RAP-status, the switching back and forth of positions and maybe more. An indication was 'work again as a people carrier', but a lazy lawyer is the worst thing that can happen! Writing a letter was all she could do. But this one was even worse than that. She had stored the file, but after the prescribed retention period she called me and said that she should have thrown it away a long time ago. She asked what I wanted to do with it. I said she could send it to another lawyer. It was kept there for a while until I picked it up some years later. If someone says that you yourself are to blame, than the question will be whether public servants are shooting with a bow and arrow all day long for the preservation of their jobs.

Anyway, this situation did not bring me down mentally. It was rather the other way around; it made me stronger. Life offers so many beautiful things, so why should I spoil it by spending too much time mobbing around about miseries brought about by others? They could keep their spuriousness to themselves.

Maybe I could continue working at the Municipality by using the we-are-going-to-sort-this-out circuit, but booth-licking was not my thing. There were also too many people 'working' on the case; where the left hand does not know what the right hand is doing. Finally, that infamous note from Tjon A Lep was still there; it would be there always, like the sword of Damocles hanging over my head.

Years later I saw some of them face to face. In relation to security issues, the security company for which I worked stationed me at the Metro. A few metro drivers said: "Finally justice has been done." Happily I greeted Mr. Green and the others who were there; Yvonne Waalders, with the widely spread legs, became chief of metro drivers; I saw Johan van Staveren, a shift leader at the subway, several times from behind a window looking around in the street where I lived. I once had a gig in front of his house during a New Year party. I spoke to Wim Boers on the square; he was doing nothing with his wife and children.

When I once encountered Boelandt shortly after the resignation, he did not know where to go; he faltered some nonsense and walked away quickly. In 2014 I saw him again. His hair had turned white and had started falling off. He was sent on early retirement and was odd jobbing. Bernard Kuyt once stood next to me in the Metro; pretending not to see me. He was also banned from the Scheepvaarthuis to the office of the union. The Mediation Team could temporarily get a room in the city hall. At the Kwakoe Festival, where I had a gig in the Antillean tent, I ran into John Tjon A Lep. "You have to watch what you sign" was all he could say. I once saw Vreede walking with a bouquet of flowers in her hands over Bijlmerplein. She also ended up in the redundancy scheme. I had heard about De Beer that this whole affair had resulted in a heart attack. I saw Swinkels once in a bar. He almost fell over from drunkenness and he could only babble. Verdam's, teeth were discolored in 2015. Out of his words, I deducted that he was not satisfied with his work at the GVB.

And let's not forget the VIC's offspring results. The legal dossier remained at home. It could be reopened if new facts were to come to light. Many of those involved, however, had passed away or could not be retraced. Besides that, they would have to testify against themselves. Would you? Nearly every day I looked at them. The civilian contract kept on triggering me big time.

15. COME WHAT MAY

I kept on wondering about the status of my employment contract under civil law and I also was curious about the contents of the file. It was messy and quite thick. After the crusade against the lawyers, I kept it at my home for a long time. I had no idea what to do with it. But on a day I opened it, looking for the ghost. That's when I got the idea to write the book 'HOEZO DISCRIMINATIE?'

But there were some spooky things going on; pathetic people who were in desperate need of attention. In a letter dated October 29, 2003, I had informed the director of the GVB that a book was coming up. This letter took a completely unexpected turn, however. It jutted out that there had been a silence about employment contract under civil law. I was still curious what the intention of the contract was in combination with the permanent appointment. But above all, I was surprised that more than 20 years after the facts, people at the GVB were still sniffing around in that old file. This is evidenced by an email from the GVB Recruitment Department dated Tuesday, July 1, 2008, 10:30 AM. It states:

"... we have gathered information from your personnel file. Here we see some tension, based on which we do not consider it appropriate to include you ..."

The file was supposed to remain sealed. It was now time to ask a few questions to the Municipality of Amsterdam. Again and again it tried to hide behind the dismissal decision of June 11, 1993. I decided to send a letter about the case to the Court of Amsterdam, Administrative Law sector. Then, a number of lawsuits followed—also at the Centrale Raad van Beroep—at the end the Cantonal Court. The consideration of the Central Council of Appeal (CRvB) read:

"In addition, the Council notes that a decision on the contract, a legal action under civil law, cannot be considered as a decision - a written decision, which includes a public legal act."
ECLI:NL:CRVB:2010:BM2232

In short, the cantonal court has jurisdiction over the employment contract, so I headed for the canton. I did not want to wait until they would come down to me. The judge showed me a direction to a very long discussion. Also the canton confirmed that I had been appointed as a civil servant, but had also received an employment relationship under civil law. I had never worked as a tram driver anyway, and that was not because of Peters' crystal ball. I suspected that the municipality refused to provide clarity about the employment contract in combination with the permanent appointment. That feeling has also been confirmed by the cantonal judge.

The Municipality was not willing to accept my point of view. Even thought I had done other work—which was more administrative in nature—prior the dismissal, it did not matter to the Municipality Amsterdam. They threw the most far-reaching argument in their plead for terms of limitation. The magistrate with this and stated on November 18, 2010:

"Grounds for the decision: On April 1, 1988 Anthony started working for the public transport company of the Municipality. He started off as a Cabin Steward, but he has subsequently performed in other functions as well. He was appointed as an official, but also received an employment relationship under civil law. Shortly before that decision (January 14, 1991), the parties has entered into an employment agreement under civil law for a period of six months commencing on January 1, 1991 ... this is the actual end of the civil contract—meant by Anthony—on the day before January 1, 1991 (the effective date of his tenure as a civil servant), or on January 14, 1991 (the date of the appropriate decision officials judge), or on the day before July 1, 1991 (the end of the agreed period). Which one of these data is correct, is no longer relevant, because it doesn't matter which date is maintained, since in any case the just-mentioned six-month limitation period— article 7: 683 Burgelijk Wetboek—had elapsed on January 1, 1992. Since the summons were not issued earlier than April 22, 2010, and it was not claimed that the limitation period was interrupted prior to January 1, 1992, it must therefore be concluded that the Municipality justifiably has invoked limitation ... Thus, the court is not allowed to receive the substantive assessment of his complaints, however much Anthony will regret. Anthony's claims will be rejected on that ground."

Fixed times; deadlines—yes, they were very important. In the light of what the court had said in its ruling in 1993: "Would want to work as people carrier again", I think that in this two-headed employment the position of desk officer, that was based on the contract under civil law, has overruled the position of tram driver. Because of these special circumstances it replaced my permanent appointment as a tram driver. That dismissal from municipal service was established by law; very logically. After all, I wasn't allowed to drive the tram ever again. My license was revoked after the decision of January 14, 1991. The actual work I was doing since January 1, 1991 was as a desk officer. After January 21, 1991, I continued in that same position while there was a permanent appointment in the position of tram driver. After July 1, 1991 (the end of the agreed period of the contract) the situation remained the same, by commonly implied consent between the Parties; me and the Municipality; albeit that it was not written on paper. It was thus a change of employment and/or change of position. As the GVB considered me to be a danger on the road, the change was for reasons of the service. A change of employment and/or position does not change the permanent appointment. The mediation was meant for a permanent work place and it couldn't be established.

In other words, I had a permanent appointment in the position of tram driver on paper, while in fact I was working as a desk officer. For me, the Municipality had generated legitimate expectations which should have been honored within the reasonability. Then for which function was the dismissal from municipality service intended? That's what it was about; nothing else. The contract came about because a permanent civil servant appointment was thwarted. But because of the harassing by a group of public servants, this contract turned out to be a failure. Many lawyers were surprised that the contract still existed, because it had never been terminated and especially because in fact I continued doing the same work; not driving a tram.

My advisor was LL.M. Garrett and in his advise on September 17, 2009 he wrote to me: "It's something else entirely that the judge's ruling in 1991 had not been followed ... I do think your letters dated 17 and March 28, 2008, can be considered as a request to take a new decision on the fact that the contract in 1991 still exists."

The purpose of this contract was to remain a mystery, highly confidential, but even with that grasp on the terms of limitation to seize the case, that larding with my legal status could also have turned out differently. That discrimination against me didn't affect me for long. As from the beginning they tried to exclude me from a job at the GVB, it was evident that a career as public servant was not feasible. Although the bond of trust was broken, I treated them friendlily, from a appropriate distance to the clog. Nowadays, I see it as a hidebound corporate culture; it looks like 'incompatibilité d'humeur' to me. In any case, I didn't lie down between the burdens. Maybe I seemed to be a bit more bold or impertinent than I ought to have been, but be pleased to consider that it wasn't my intention. "I'm so sorry, it wasn't meant that way."

Since January 1, 2007, the GVB has been a privatized transport company. The sole shareholder till now is the city of Amsterdam.

ABOUT THE AUTHOR

Julino Willem Anthony was born on February 23, 1956 on Bonaire. There he attended primary school and then the LTS. This 4 years education was completed in Curaçao. This was followed by a company training at Shell Curaçao N.V.

The love for singing began at an early age. In Curacao, he further developed this passion.
Under the stage name William Anthony, he has performed at many venues as a singer and released a number of CDs independently. He sometimes also had a gig as actor and (noble) extra in Dutch television productions.

These and all the other artistic experiences are written in his book 'Musika Maestro'. The first edition appeared in 2002. The second edition has been updated in 2014 and the English edition has been published in 2015. From the author appeared in 2014 the prose book in Papiamento SOBRÁ. This all shows William Anthony's versatility.

In 1986 William Anthony moved to the Netherlands. In 'Why Discrimination?' he tells about his experiences with discrimination and how he dealt with the culture shock.

These activities happens in addition to his regular job.

Furthermore, he enjoys what life has to offer.

www.ingramcontent.com/pod-product-compliance
Lightning Source LLC
Chambersburg PA
CBHW071213280526
45787CB00002B/660